SWITZERLAND:
a Cartoon Survival Guide

Switzerland: a Cartoon Survival Guide

© 2017 Schwabe AG, Bergli Books, Basel

© 2017 Sergio J. Lievano and Wolfgang Koydl

Published by
Bergli Books
Imprint of Schwabe AG
www.bergli.ch

Printed in Switzerland by Schwabe AG, Muttenz

Der Verlag Bergli Books wird vom Bundesamt für Kultur mit einem Strukturbeitrag für die Jahre 2016-2018 unterstützt.

ISBN 978-3-03869-021-4

This book is also available in German as

Ganz schön Schweiz: ein Cartoon Survival Guide
ISBN 978-3-03869-022-1

SWITZERLAND: a Cartoon Survival Guide

by

Sergio J. Lievano

Wolfgang Koydl

Table of Contents

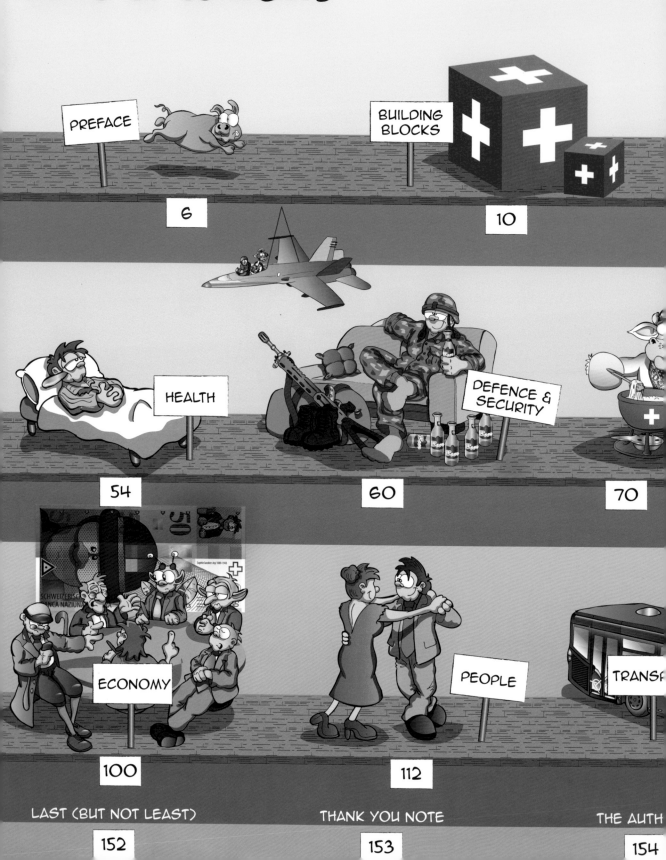

PREFACE

All for One...

Switzerland is not a big place, only about 40 000 square kilometres all told, including lakes and rivers. For heaven's sake, there are counties that size. Elko, for instance, in the US state of Nevada, covers about the same area as Switzerland.

Switzerland languishes down at place 132 on a list of 195 nations ranked by size – just above Bhutan and Guinea-Bissau.

However, you'd be hard pressed to find anyone who hasn't heard about that rich little country in the Alps: mountains, cows, chocolate, cheese, watches, peace, brotherhood and neutrality. Or, depending on your preferences: tax shelters, money laundering, slush funds and tacit support for third-world dictators.

Regardless of whether you focus on the good, the bad or the ugly, Switzerland usually punches above its weight. Here, small is not only beautiful, but powerful, as well.

Examples? The Swiss have one of the world's strongest currencies and can claim the only first class university outside Britain or America. They generate more wealth per capita than Japan or Germany, are among the top 20 exporting nations, and rank number three world-wide in new patents registered.

Swiss diplomacy works quietly to resolve conflicts – being small and neutral has advantages. The Red Cross, the United Nations and the International Olympic Committee all have headquarters here. To say nothing of the International Federation of Sports Chiropractic.

There's soft cultural power, too: readers everywhere know the orphan girl Heidi or the equally indomitable Swiss Family Robinson. Design and architecture are unthinkable without Swiss contributions: Le Corbusier invented modern buildings, while Max Miedinger and Adrian Frutiger created the timeless fonts Helvetica and, well, Frutiger.

This success is even more notable if one considers that Switzerland lacks many of the attributes a well-functioning state should have. A poor peasant society surrounded by stronger, predatory powers – in Europe this was usually a shortcut to oppression, occupation or annihilation.

Add the fact that Switzerland is a lose patchwork of 26 bickering, proud and independent cantons, historically divided by language and religion and lacking strong central authority, only divine providence seems to be able to explain its continued existence.

While it is true that most people have some notion about the Swiss, few have any real knowledge. Winston Churchill's dictum about Russia being "a riddle wrapped in a mystery inside an enigma" could apply to Switzerland, too – if Europeans cared to take a closer look at their mysterious neighbour.

Instead, they see it as a boring little country, an Alpine paradise, a bankers' vault or a xenophobic mountain fortress, populated by people as diverse as tennis super star Roger Federer and football super rascal Sepp Blatter. A nation made up in equal measure of clean, punctual model citizens and petty-minded, penny-pinching control-freaks.

The Swiss are all of this – but they're also much, much more. They're weird, sexy, radical and at times even funny. Their German is incomprehensible to other German-speakers, their national games are inscrutable, and their sex lives put passionate southern Europeans to shame.

Especially their political system is unlike any other – so radical and egalitarian, it would be a New Hampshire libertarian's dream come true. Switzerland has no capital, no prime minister, not even a government in the usual sense. Instead, the people rule: parliamentary decisions are subject to approval by the voters.

Our book tries to rectify this gap in knowledge. There's much to learn about Switzerland, still more to make you marvel, puzzle, wonder or even laugh. The Swiss could be an example: how to make money, how to organize a society, how to live well and contentedly – they're pretty good at all of these things. Unfortunately, they are too shy and modest to blow their own horn.

This is where we come in. Sergio and myself don't claim to be the ultimate Swiss experts. I doubt that anyone will ever gauge the depths of the Swiss soul.

But we've become quite Swissified. Sergio still hasn't given up hope that one day he will bring the light of Swiss reason to his native Colombia. As for myself, I grieve when I see that Switzerland still has all the attributes my own home country of Germany once had – and lost.

We hope that at the end of our book you will be wiser than that German ex-president, who had Switzerland patiently explained to him. "I think, I may have some idea now," he eventually exclaimed. "But I don't understand how such a country could ever work."

...and
One for All

SWISS MOTTO

*The Musketeers were swashbuckling daredevils – not exactly the image that springs to mind for the staid Swiss. And yet, they pinched the Frenchmen's motto: "One for all, and all for one" is Switzerland's unofficial slogan. The Latin version "**Unus pro omnibus, omnes pro uno**" graces a mosaic in parliament.*

BUILDING BLOCKS

THE NAME

Regardless if you say Switzerland, Suisse or Schweiz – it's just a convenience. It stems from canton Schwyz, named after a Celtic leader called **Suito** *and the name was long considered offensive by other Swiss. The official name is* **Confoederatio Helvetica** *– Latin for Swiss Confederation. Latin makes sense in a country that speaks four languages.*

When trying to gauge the inscrutable Swiss, one could do worse than comparing them to their watches: both are reliable, unostentatious, and not cheap. And, oh yes, the better ones are very complicated.

Like a Swiss watch, the Swiss nation is made up of many different components. A French speaking banker on Geneva's elegant Rue du Rhone has little in common with a vintner toiling in a breathtakingly steep vineyard a few miles away on the shores of Lake Geneva. Yet both differ again from a worker in a watch factory in the Jura mountains, a fashionable receptionist on her Vespa in Lugano, or a famous scientist at Zurich's prestigious technical college.

But just as the screws, springs and balance wheels interlock to bring a watch to life, so do all these different people work together to make the country tick. Viewed under a magnifying glass, they're all individual pieces, yet together they make one remarkably well-functioning whole.

There are one or two commonalities, however, which shape Swiss people's character: nature and heritage. Most Swiss are descended from peasant stock. Often, you don't even have to look far to find an ancestor who worked the land. More often than not, his homestead would have been in some rocky, inhospitable valley, where unpredictable weather turned agriculture into a perilous gamble.

This made people cautious, frugal and quite wary, too. They had to adapt, improvise and compromise. They needed their wits about them for practical things. A grand vision doesn't get your family through winter after a bad harvest. And: your own people always come first – your family, your village, your valley, your canton, and eventually your country.

This is the foundation upon which Switzerland is built.

Planet Switzerland

THE FLAG

Unique, square, instantly recognizable. Stands for solidity, security, stability and neutrality. Saudi Arabia didn't like it on the fuselage of Swiss planes: a cross in the sky.

THE FONT

Helvetica

No matter where you live, no matter what you stare at, It's probably written in a Swiss font

THE SCIENCE

Einstein learnt his bag of tricks in Zurich. Today's places of educational excellence hide behind acronyms: ETH, EPLF, CERN, HSG.

$E=MC^2$

THE FOOD

If it contains cheese or cream, it's probably a Swiss dish.

Nature, both grand and sweet, invites all things
[outd]oors: skiing, hiking, running, swimming, barbecuing.

THE LAND

THE PEOPLE

Proud, free and independent. They hold
the power in the land. Full stop.

THE SUPERPOWER

Politically a midget, Switzerland dwarves
many bigger countries in terms of trade,
output and GDP.

THE MOUNTAIN

Just what a mountain should look like.
Matterhorn is up there with Mount
Fuji and Kilimanjaro.

THE NEUTRALITY

Forced on the Swiss, but
[s]ubsequently kept them out of
[tr]ouble and always made them
a tidy little bundle.

THE PRODUCT

Watches, sure. No cuckoo clocks,
but much more, too. Prepare
to be surprised.

THE ARTS

Yes, he's Swiss, but Alberto "The Stickman"
Giacometti is only one of many international artists to
have called Switzerland home.

THE FLAG

The world's only square flag apart from the Vatican, it was first flown in the battle of Laupen in 1339 when central Swiss cantons and mighty Bern needed a common sign. It quickly became accepted as Switzerland's official flag, but only received its final form in 1889.

The arms of the Swiss cross are not as long as they are wide, but one sixth longer. It looks better this way.

THE "CH" THING...

Not even the pope would put Latin on his country's number plates. That is the prerogative of the Swiss. Their country code on the back of cars is CH – the abbreviation of the official Latin name **Confoederatio Helvetica**.

Switzerland in Numbers

ZURICH
(not the capital)

NEIGHBOURS
Germany, France, Italy, Austria and tiny little Liechtenstein

BERN
(a capital - of sorts)

French
22.5%

German
63.9%

GENEVA
(also, not the capital)

Italian
8.1%

Romansh
0.5%

AREA
41 285 km²
(between the Netherlands and Taiwan)

CANTONS
26

TOURISM
49.5 million air passengers and CHF 47.8 billion generated just in 2015

FEMALE
50.5%

RURAL POPULATION
26.2%

IMMIGRATION

40 000 (2016)

SWISS ABROAD
8.9% (France destination No. 1)

DIVERSITY

The Swiss are not a single ethnic group but made up of various nationalities, shaped by their German, French and Italian neighbours. They're only held together by their common will to be a nation.

GDP PER CAPITA

CHF 80 200 (2016)

NUMBER OF COWS

1.59 million

POPULATION
8 391 973

SWISS
75.7%

FOREIGNERS
24.3% (as percentage of total population)

BIRTH RATE
1.54 kids per woman

DENSITY
198 people/km²

LIFE EXPECTANCY
82.70 years

MALE
49.5%

HELVETIA

Sister of Britannia, Germania or Bavaria, she was born in the 1600s as an all-encompassing allegorical figure behind whom all Swiss could unite.

NOISE

Silence may be Switzerland's natural state, but don't be deceived. When they have a valid reason, the Swiss relish noise as much as anyone. Give them a task – plus a jackhammer, a leafblower, a garbage truck or any other piece of machinery and decibels soar. Given the generally low noise level, the impact on your ear-drums is disproportionately high.

HISTORY

If you are a small country somewhere in Europe, chances are pretty slim that you managed to survive all those centuries of warfare, revolutions and occupations in one piece.

Except Switzerland, which has had approximately the same geographical shape as today for hundreds of years. It got its final form in 1815 at the Congress of Vienna, but even before that the outlines looked remarkably similar. Only island nations like Britain, Ireland or Iceland have achieved a similar feat – and the latter two were under foreign rule for centuries.

The Swiss – or more precisely their cantons – have been free from outside tutelage since 1291(with one brief exception in 1798), when three communities in remote Alpine valleys united to form the **Eidgenossenschaft**, literally the "sworn confraternity".

Since then, the Swiss have had neither lord nor king nor emperor. Their peasants and burghers ruled themselves in a stubborn, boorish, but generally successful way. Sometimes they were simply regarded as eccentric by their European neighbours, sometimes as a dangerous democratic role model for their citizens and therefore a threat. This goes some way to explain the problems which Brussels and the European Union currently have with the Swiss.

Since 1515, the Swiss have not participated in European wars. This, and the absence of any memorable leaders, gave rise to the notion that Switzerland had one of the most boring histories imaginable.

Looking at the hundreds of millions of Europeans killed, maimed, displaced and dispossessed, though, the Swiss see nothing terribly wrong with that.

Multilingualism

Historically, there have always been nations where several languages were spoken. But most were sprawling empires or tightly-run nation states where other tongues were marginalized. But Switzerland accords truly equal rights to all its languages.

LOMBARDS
(600 AD)

Yet more Germanic people. They took a detour via Hungary to reach Northern Italy where in 570 they established a kingdom and spread out into the Alps' Southern foothills into present-day Ticino. With civilisation, the Langobards (literally: Longbeards) acquired Latin, too.

Switzerl

ALEMANNI
(400 AD)

Their name just means "men", but these swept down from Northern Germany a obliterate Rome's crumbling defences. established themselves around 400 AD wide area around Lake Constance and Switzerland's Celtic tribes first into mountains and then into oblivion

ROMANS
(200 BC)

Blame the Romans: After adding the Po valley to their republic around 200 BC, they conquered the Alpine valleys. After they left, their legionaries' coarse Latin stayed behind and formed the base for modern Romansh dialects.

THE HELVETII
(400 BC)

Trickling in from the early 400s BC, this eponymous Celtic tribe was first mentioned by Greek historian Poseidonios as "rich in gold, but peaceful" – which sounds about right. Became heavily Romanized and could not withstand the Alemannic onslaught after Rome left in 401 AD.

RGUNDIANS
(400 AD)

Germanic tribe of Richard Wagner's "Ring" cycle fame. But they succumbed to southern pleasures and accents once they settled in present-day France – whence they brought Francais and savoir-vivre to Western Switzerland.

RHAETIANS
(600 BC)

Mysterious original inhabitants of the Alpine region. Maybe descended from Etruscans who were driven from their native Tuscany by the Romans. Their language survives in some place names, most notably the river Rhine.

NEWCOMERS
(SINCE 1960S)

The country may be multilingual, but in their everyday dealings with each other, many French, German and Italian speaking Swiss prefer to converse in English. This also helps with large immigrant communities. Albanian, English and Portuguese are major languages spoken in the country today.

Today, 20.9% of Swiss residents speak a mother tongue that is not one of the 4 national languages. In 1970 it was 3.7 %

4.6% of Swiss speak English as a mother tongue.

THE ROMANS...

If it weren't for the Romans, Helvetia probably would be found somewhere in the South of France. Julius Caesar prevented the Celtic tribe of the Helvetii from leaving their homeland in the mountains. By and large, the six hundred years of Roman rule proved to be a boon for the country. Roads, theatres, spas and no more serious fighting: glorious pax romana.

MERCENARY ECONOMY

No money, no Swiss: this motto was the basis for a lucrative – and bloody – business that lasted almost 500 years: around one million Swiss mercenaries fought for anyone in Europe who could afford to hire them. Bern banned the custom in 1859, but only in 1929 was it made a criminal offense. Today, the only remaining Swiss guard belongs to the pope.

Poverty, overpopulation and the promise of adventure and plunder enticed peasant boys to take up arms for foreign rulers. They were highly sought after, as Swiss fighters had a reputation for courage, ruthlessness and cruelty. Some Swiss families acquired wealth and foreign titles for renting out stable boys as soldiers of fortune.

In the Middle Ages, these Swiss revolutionised warfare. Their "Gewalthaufen" – a wild throng of variously armed foot soldiers – broke up formations of mounted knights. Their weapon of choice was the halberd – an unwieldy forerunner of the multi-purpose Swiss army knife: a 1.5 metre long shaft with an axe blade and a hook, topped with a spike. It enabled them to pull riders off their noble steeds, then stab or hack at them at leisure. The Vatican Swiss guard still have them.

Rütli Oath

EIDGENOSSENSCHAFT

A foundation myth straight out of Hollywood: one man representing each of the cantons Uri, Schwyz and Unterwalden, meet on a summer's day in 1291 in a clearing over Lake Lucerne. Walter Fürst, Werner Stauffacher and Arnold Melchtal swear an oath to defend the other cantons against the beastly Hapsburg oppressors.

Missing from this event in the Rütli meadow was the man considered to be Switzerland's mythical founding father: William Tell. None of it probably ever happened the way it is described in text books. But the Rütli Oath is the nation's founding myth. **Eidgenossenschaft**, the official name, literally translates as oath-confraternity.

WILLIAM TELL

William Tell, who is said to have opposed foreign oppressors when he shot an apple from his son's head with a crossbow, is completely fictional and anything but Swiss. The legend is Danish, was turned into a play by a German author and into an opera by an Italian composer.

WHERE'S WALLY ?

Swiss parliamentarians can gaze at a naked woman in the clouds while sitting in chambers. She was hidden there by painter Charles Giron in his monumental painting to symbolize peace.

1st August

WHY 1ST AUGUST ?

Since nobody knows the exact date of the Rütli Oath, the arbitrary choice of August 1st as the national holiday was decreed by the government in 1889. But it took until 1993 to become a work-free day everywhere in Switzerland. The 16th century historian Aegidius Tschudi placed the meeting of the first three cantons on the Wednesday before St. Martins – 8 November. But then, fireworks and BBQs work so much better in summer than in winter. Just ask the Americans.

NATIONAL ANTHEM

Some are rousing, some bloodcurdling. Some are full of pathos, others just pathetic. But the Swiss national anthem is different. Mocked as a cross between a hymn and a weather report for its frequent allusions to God and meteorological phenomena, it is a rather plodding piece of music, appropriately called the **Schweizerpsalm** – the "Hymn of the Swiss."

Written in the 1840s, it was only made the official anthem in 1981. Before that, the Swiss sang something else – to the tune of **God Save The Queen**. Embarrassing mix-ups forced a change.

AND NOW, LET US SING TOGETHER OUR BELOVED NATIONAL ANTHEM !

PERHAPS WE SHOULD WAIT A LITTLE BEFORE ASKING FOR MONEY TO BUY MORE FIREWORKS

A WORD OF CAUTION

Fireworks cause 250 accidents a year in Switzerland, half of them on August 1st, Swiss National Day, according to the Swiss Council for Accident Prevention.

HÖHENFEUER

Huge, metres-high pyres are lit on mountain-tops. Rumoured to commemorate the burning castles of expelled nobles.

THE LYRICS

Even though nobody is quite happy with the national anthem, numerous attempts to reform the lyrics have gone nowhere. A brand new text, recently chosen in a national competition, is less popular than the original.

NATIONAL SAUSAGE

Every year, the Swiss devour 160 million sausages called Cervelat. An unknown, but undoubtedly substantial, number of them ends up on grills for national holiday.

A nation forged in battles

Switzerland is a small and peaceful little nation that wouldn't even harm its tiny neighbour Liechtenstein. Its history, however, was bloody, violent and full of cruelty. It is fair to say that the modern country's identity and borders were forged by wars and battles – most of them won, but some also lost.

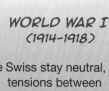

WORLD WAR I (1914–1918)

The Swiss stay neutral, but tensions between French-leaning Romands and Kaiser-loving Swiss Germans almost come to a boil.

SWABIAN WARS (1499)

WORLD WAR II (1939–1945)

Switzerland is surrounded by Fascist powers. Hitler muses how to "squeeze that zit on Europe's face". The Swiss survive by being nice to everyone.

A bunch of mountain yokels defeats a few thousand Hapsburg knights. The peasants use whatever is at hand – pitchforks, logs rolled down slopes and boulders thrown by strong arms. A nearby lake helps to drown survivors.

BATTLE OF MORGARTEN (1315) DAVID VS GOLIATH 2.0

NAPOLEONIC WARS (1798)

Napoleon Bonaparte visits the long-time provider of mercenaries – and stays.

His troops occupy the country and establish the **Helvetic Republic**, a rigidly centralized state along French li...

It lasts only till 1803.

COLD WAR 1949–1989

Reagan and Gorbachev bury the hatchet in supposedly neutral Geneva, but tacitly Switzerland had always been considered part of the West. Since the end of the Cold War the country has become somewhat untethered, as the EU is not considered an option by many.

SONDERBUNDKRIEG (1847)

The last religious war on Swiss soil lasts three weeks and mercifully only claims 150 lives, but it establishes Protestant dominance in the new Confederation for years to come.

BATTLE OF SEMPACH (1386)

The Hapsburgs get another drubbing and the Swiss acquire their first national martyr – Arnold von Winkelried throws himself bare-chested into a phalanx of enemy spears, cutting a swathe for his comrades' attack.

BURGUNDIAN WARS (1476)

...fter losing all Swiss lands, the Hapsburgs come back for one last try. But even though they're helped by Swabian ...ercenaries – who coin the expletive **Cow Swiss** – they're routed for good. The Swiss add Ticino and Milan to their possessions.

Having expelled the Hapsburgs, the Swiss face a powerful new foe in the West. Charles the Bold, Duke of Burgundy (not related to Ron Burgundy), is felled in battle by a single halberd-wielding peasant. Switzerland becomes a major European power.

BATTLE OF MARIGNANO (1515)

...ilan proves to be a conquest too much. First major Swiss defeat, at the hands of the French who henceforth become premium customers for Swiss mercenaries. End of Swiss military expansion.

KAPPELER WARS (1529)

Like the rest of Europe, the Swiss find religion a good reason to smash each other's heads in. Wars repeatedly pit Catholics and Protestants against each other. The Kappel one ends on an unusually friendly note when both sides share a kettle of milk soup.

Bad Memories

The Swiss are rightly proud of who they are, what they are, and how they got there. But as in any nation, they have some skeletons in their historical closet, which they prefer to keep hidden.

It's one of the most infamous quotes used to fend off people in need: "The boat is full." It was coined by Swiss minister Eduard von Steiger in August 1942. Speaking at a Christian brass music festival, he defended the government's decision to close borders to Jews fleeing from the Nazis. Persecution on racial grounds was no longer a reason for granting asylum.

If you really want to knock the Swiss out of their stride, innocently ask to be reminded when their women received the right to vote. Today, most Swiss - men included - consider it as a stain on their reputation that it took until 1971 for their mothers, wives, sisters, daughters and girlfriends to fully participate in political decision-making. In canton Appenzell it took two decades more. The lame excuse back in the old days: protect women from political parties.

WOMEN'S VOTE

JEWS IN WORLD WAR II

GROUNDING

INDENTURED CHILD LABOUR

They were exploited, beaten, starved of affection and of food: between the 1920s and as late as the early 1970s, more than 100 000 boys and girls were placed, against their parents' will, with foster families. Mostly, these were poor farmers who needed **Verdingkinder** (literally: contract children) as cheap labour. Only recently, has this abuse been made public. An initiative has been set in motion to compensate the surviving 10 000 child labourers from a 500-million-franc fund.

A brief announcement at Zurich airport shook the nation to the core, and the trauma has not been forgotten: "due to financial reasons, Swissair is unable to execute any of its flights", the speaker declared on October 2, 2001. The 71-year-old airline, the nation's pride and glory, had gone into receivership. With all its planes grounded and 19 000 passengers stranded, the world witnessed scenes of panic and incompetence not seen in Switzerland before or – luckily – ever since.

wiss like Napoleon III, who was
ss citizen, but their relationship
vith Napoleon Bonaparte is
iguous. You rarely hear that he
uered, occupied and reshaped
Federation twice: once like a
h department, the second time
e embarrassingly – he moulded
modern Swiss state. In other
ds: Their republic was helped
by an emperor's not so gentle
nudge.

Proud of their own democratic
pedigree, Swiss mercenaries
nevertheless defended vile
autocrats: Lucerne's Lion
Monument commemorates the
death of almost 1000 Swiss
guards who were killed
defending Louis XVI against
French revolutionaries in 1792.
Half a century later, Swiss
soldiers helped Ferdinand II, last
king of the Two Sicilies, to
violently suppress a revolt by his
own people.

The Swiss trust their
government inherently.
Imagine the shock when it
was revealed in 1989 that the
state had snooped on its
citizens for years and kept
secret files on more than
900 000 of them. The **Fichen
Scandal** shattered
confidence in state
institutions for years to come.

MERCENARIES

LEON

SECRET
FILES

PROTESTANT
TALIBAN

Jean Calvin and Huldrych Zwingli were notable
Protestant reformers, but their theocratic regimes
in Geneva and Zurich bore more than a passing
resemblance to the Islamic State: heretics and
other opponents were ruthlessly persecuted,
tortured and even killed. Calvin personally
approved the burning at the stake of Spanish
humanist Michael Servetus.

BANKING
SECRECY

An aura surrounds Swiss banks, but sometimes it's
more like a stench. Behind those polished
mahogany doors the famed Swiss banking secrecy
hid many dirty secrets as well as dirty money
stashed away by crooks, dictators or tax evaders.
In the 1990s, a spotlight was turned on dormant
Jewish accounts whose existence the banks had
hidden since WW II. The code of secrecy only
collapsed in 2012 when parliament – faced by the
threat of crippling penalties to the banks – agreed
to pass information to U.S. authorities.

GEOGRAPHY

One of the best jokes in the Swiss adventure of the legendary cartoon duo Asterix and Obelix comes at the end of the book. Big, bumbling Obelix – who was out cold for most of the journey – is asked how he's finding Switzerland. He shrugs, draws a straight line with his hand, and says: "Flat."

This is funny because everyone knows that Switzerland is all about mountains. They shape and define its geography, its mentality and the outside world's idea of the country. This is best summed up by the Matterhorn: ask a kid to draw a mountain, it would look like the Matterhorn.

But there's much more to Switzerland than majestic ranges and frozen peaks: glittering lakes, carved out by glaciers and lined by ancient cities are integral to Switzerland as well. Actually, mountains, lake and town make for the perfect Swiss trifecta. Think Zurich, Geneva, Lucerne or Lugano.

Then there are broad and fertile valleys, traversed by mighty rivers. Two of Europe's most important waterways – the Rhone and the Rhine – have their headwaters in Switzerland. Rolling hills and lush meadows vie with craggy rock outcrops.

This diversity – and the need to circumnavigate some forbidding peak – makes Switzerland appear much bigger than it is. Sometimes it feels as if there were two different countries on different sides of a mountain.

Contrary to some beliefs, the Swiss have not quite achieved their objective of completing a maze of tunnels that would enable travellers to cross the whole country underground.

Mountains

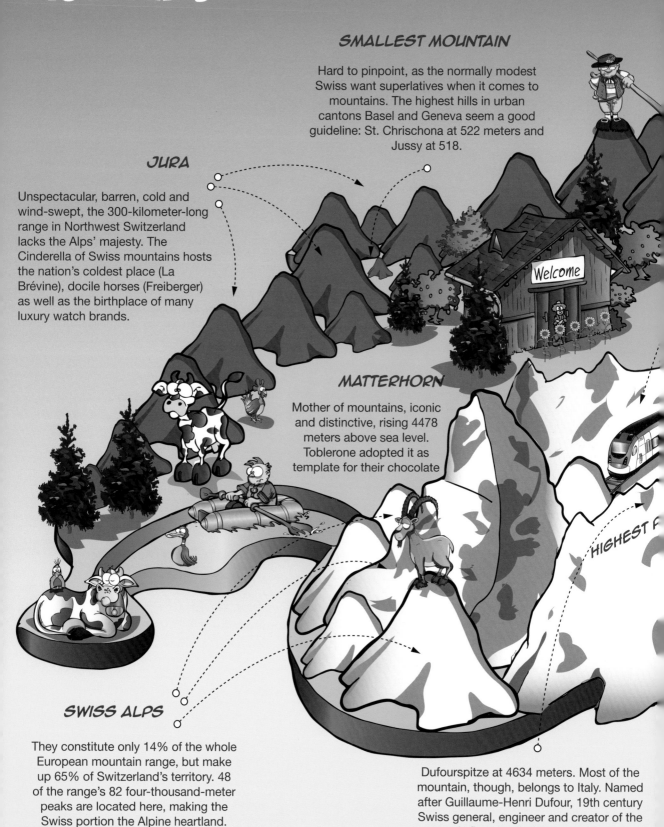

SMALLEST MOUNTAIN

Hard to pinpoint, as the normally modest Swiss want superlatives when it comes to mountains. The highest hills in urban cantons Basel and Geneva seem a good guideline: St. Chrischona at 522 meters and Jussy at 518.

JURA

Unspectacular, barren, cold and wind-swept, the 300-kilometer-long range in Northwest Switzerland lacks the Alps' majesty. The Cinderella of Swiss mountains hosts the nation's coldest place (La Brévine), docile horses (Freiberger) as well as the birthplace of many luxury watch brands.

MATTERHORN

Mother of mountains, iconic and distinctive, rising 4478 meters above sea level. Toblerone adopted it as template for their chocolate

Welcome

HIGHEST F

SWISS ALPS

They constitute only 14% of the whole European mountain range, but make up 65% of Switzerland's territory. 48 of the range's 82 four-thousand-meter peaks are located here, making the Swiss portion the Alpine heartland.

Dufourspitze at 4634 meters. Most of the mountain, though, belongs to Italy. Named after Guillaume-Henri Dufour, 19th century Swiss general, engineer and creator of the country's first detailed topographical map.

EIGER, MÖNCH AND JUNGFRAU

An Alpine theme park. Cricket, soccer and tennis have all been played here for PR purposes. One of the first mountains opened up to tourism, thanks to a cog railroad that takes visitors to Europe's highest railway station (3454 meters). Chinese tourists find the world's highest watch shop, while Indians enjoy curries at the Bollywood restaurant.

GLARUS

Some inhabitants describe feeling like they live in a long, dark corridor, as most of the canton is located in a narrow valley with sheer rock faces rising on either side.

Myth and legend, stony fortress and gateway to the South, the Gotthard and its pass hold a special place in Swiss hearts. This usually turns to heart-burn during holidays, when traffic jams clog the road before the tunnel.

GOTTHARD

LOWEST POINT

The Dead Sea it isn't. At 193 meters above sea level, Lago Maggiore in Ticino is still pretty high. It actually dwarfs Mollehoj, Denmark's highest "mountain" by 23 meters.

THE HEART OF DARKNESS

For three months in winter – November till January – no ray of sun reaches the village of Bosco Gurin in Ticino, which is hidden behind high mountains. More than a dozen hamlets in Switzerland share this fate, albeit not quite that long.

AGRICULTURE

Postcard perfect Swiss landscapes convey the image of a bucolic idyll where hardworking farmers plough their fields and tend their flocks. The ever-present sound of cowbells only reaffirms this view. Reality, however, is less romantic.

While the one million hectares of farmland cover about a fourth of the country's total area, there are only 55 000 farms left, employing just 158 000 people. On average, farmers earn 40 000 francs a year and need government help: 2.8 billion francs are paid each year to the agricultural sector, which contributes scarcely more than one percent to GDP.

... DISTURBING THE PEACE...

KLING!

KLANG!

KLANG!

KLING!

KLING!

OUTDOORS

Other nations may have palaces, temples or battle fields as tokens of their identity. The Swiss have a meadow. There's nothing special about that small patch of green overlooking Lake Lucerne, where three oath-brothers met. Yet, the outdoors location is quite symbolic, since favourite Swiss pastimes happen out of doors: hiking, biking, picnic and barbeques. The indoors still inspire some oaths: never to drink that much beer again, or lose some weight before the next hike.

Outdoors

SKIING

The Swiss quickly copied mad[?]
Englishmen, who introduced
skiing in the 1800s. St. Moritz
claims to be the birthplace
of winter tourism (1864).
Davos installed the
first T-bar ski-lift in 1934.

BASEJUMPING

With 20 000 jumps per year, Lauterbrunnen
in canton Bern tops the list worldwide.
Unfortunately, with around 40 deaths,
it's also number one for fatalities.

SWIMMING

Mostly done in lakes or rivers. Outdo[?]
pools – called **Badis** – are located he[?]
A must in Bern: the **Aare Schwumm**[?]
leisurely float along the river.

OPEN AIR EVENTS

Mostly in summer one can find,
among others: cinema, operas,
theatres and concerts

HIKING

Hostile powers should invade Switzerland on a sunny
Sunday afternoon – when everybody is on a hike
in the countryside. More Swiss than yodelling:
45 percent of the population describe
themselves as regular hikers.

COW ESCAPING

Not an outdoor activity per se, but
indeed something to bear in mind when
hiking or biking. Statistically, cows are
deadlier than sharks so it is wise to
keep out of their path

MOUNTAINEERING

Early British mountaineers needed local sherpas and found them in Swiss villages. In 1863, the Swiss Alpine Club (SAC) was founded. Today it has 145 000 members and maintains 152 mountain huts.

BIRDWATCHING

(see **Wildlife** page)

MOUNTAIN BIKING

land offers endless
ns when riding a
from city tours to
enturous alpine trails.

TRAILS

65 000 kilometres of hiking trails, from Easy strolls to demanding mountain tours. Distances are given in hours, not kilometres. If you're late, you must be lost.

ACT NORMAL...!

NAKED HIKING

Still a niche pastime. Shoes and hats are a must, everything else should be exposed to the elements and curious glances.

In 2011, Switzerland's highest court ruled canton Apenzell had the right to fine those who partake.

Cities

Exactly 88 towns qualify as cities, i.e. they have a population exceeding 10 000. This elevates unfamiliar places such as Pully, Grenchen or Cham to this category. Only six cities have more than 100 000 inhabitants. Number one is Zurich with 400 000 – just as big as Wichita, Kansas or Wuppertal in Germany.

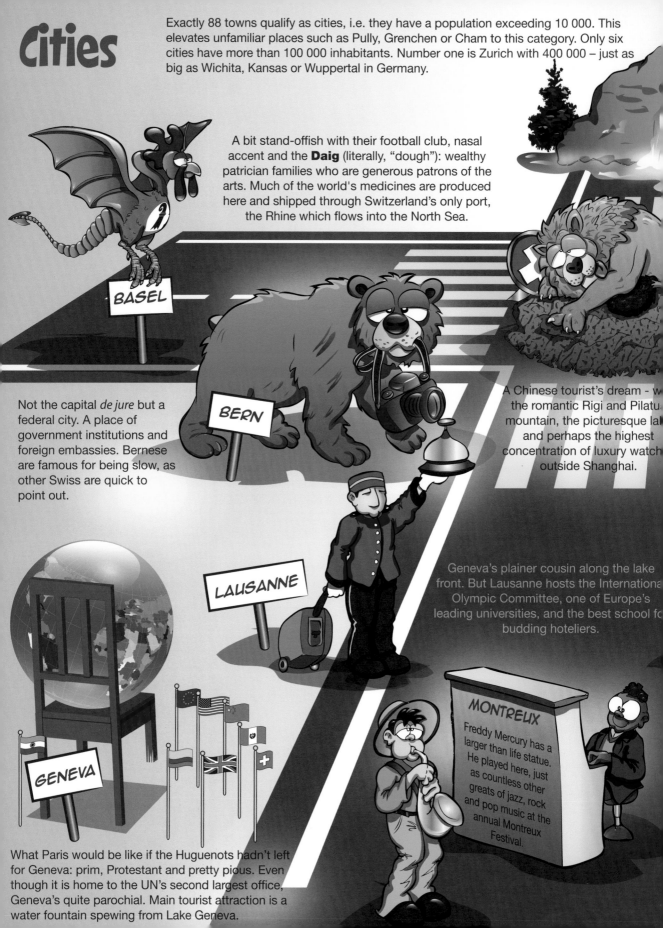

A bit stand-offish with their football club, nasal accent and the **Daig** (literally, "dough"): wealthy patrician families who are generous patrons of the arts. Much of the world's medicines are produced here and shipped through Switzerland's only port, the Rhine which flows into the North Sea.

BASEL

BERN

Not the capital *de jure* but a federal city. A place of government institutions and foreign embassies. Bernese are famous for being slow, as other Swiss are quick to point out.

A Chinese tourist's dream - w the romantic Rigi and Pilatu mountain, the picturesque la and perhaps the highest concentration of luxury watch outside Shanghai.

LAUSANNE

Geneva's plainer cousin along the lake front. But Lausanne hosts the Internationa Olympic Committee, one of Europe's leading universities, and the best school fo budding hoteliers.

GENEVA

MONTREUX

Freddy Mercury has a larger than life statue. He played here, just as countless other greats of jazz, rock and pop music at the annual Montreux Festival.

What Paris would be like if the Huguenots hadn't left for Geneva: prim, Protestant and pretty pious. Even though it is home to the UN's second largest office, Geneva's quite parochial. Main tourist attraction is a water fountain spewing from Lake Geneva.

Switzerland's northernmost town, it guards the nearby Rhine Falls, Europe's largest waterfall. Due to its location next to the German border, it suffered serious damage when bombed by the Allies in WW II.

SCHAFFHAUSEN

ZURICH

In German, "zu" means "too" as in too much, so Switzerland's biggest city is considered zu rich, as well as zu arrogant, zu smug and zu fast talking by other Swiss.

LUCERNE

The Irish monk St. Gallus first lived here in a hermit's hut. His ecclesiastical successors were not so modest. Their splendid abbey was one of the richest in Europe.

ST. GALL

World Concern...ish

BELLINZONA

DAVOS

The town's three castles always held the key to Italy. Smaller than Lugano, it's still the canton's capital. Well known to Switzerland's gangsters, as it hosts the supreme criminal court.

LOCARNO

Europe's highest city at 1560 meters. Gained fame as destination for TB sufferers in the 19th century. Now home of "Davos Man", a species best observed in its habitat, the annual World Economic Forum.

It attracted assorted artists who 100 years ago founded an anarchist, nudist, vegetarian and communal utopian cooperative colony on Monte Verità. Today, movie celebrities flock to the film festival.

Lakes

Compared to Finland with 187 888 lakes, the number of Switzerland's roughly 1400 bodies of water is puny. Yet, Switzerland's lakes are as iconic as the mountains.

LAKE GENEVA

Almost a sea with 580 square kilometres, of which 60% are Swiss. One of the few lakes featured in rock music: Deep Purple's "Smoke on the Water" commemorates a fire at the Montreux casino.

LAKE NEUCHATEL

At 218 square kilometres, Switzerland's largest lake within the borders.

WATER QUALITY

The water quality of the Swiss lakes has been improving since 1970 – all have been declared safe for swimming.

LAKE BRIENZ

The steep rock faces make it look like a Norwegian fjord.

LAKE LUGANO

It emerged after two glaciers crashed headlong before melting. Opposite the city of Lugano is a little piece of Italy: the exclave of Campione.

Casino

LAKE LUCERNE

The cradle of the Confederation: in the Rütli Meadow the first three cantons declared their freedom. The fictional freedom fighter William Tell nearly drowned in one of the lake's notorious Föhn storms – a meteorological phenomenon that is enjoyed by wind surfers today.

LAGO MAGGIORE

...eatured in Ernest Hemingway's **A Farewell to Arms**. Two ...mantic holiday destinations are located here: Ascona and Locarno.

LAKE ZURICH

Some of the richest and most famous people in the world live on its shores: Tina Turner, Roger Federer and assorted oligarchs.

GREIFENSEE

Small, calm and idyllic little lake near Zurich. Its shores are unspoilt by buildings – with few exceptions like medieval Greifensee Castle.

LAKE ST. MORITZ

There's water polo and there's polo, but what about playing a few chukkas on a lake? The lake in Switzerland's swankiest resort is the venue for a polo tournament. In winter, naturally, when the lake is frozen.

Strictly speaking two lakes with a connecting river, the Rhine. Shared with Germany and Austria

ZOLL DOUANE

ZOLL DOUANE

LAKE CONSTANCE

FAUNA & FLORA

Let other nations display fierce predators as symbols of their identity – the English lion, the American eagle, the Russian bear. The Swiss, alas, are neither fierce nor predatory. If they ever were in need of a heraldic animal, it would have to be the docile cow. No other animal is so much associated with Switzerland as the quietly masticating milk-machine.

There's one cow for every ten people; three times as many bovine, once calves, bulls and oxen are included. They seem to be everywhere and they assault all your senses: you see them, hear their bells, and their cowpats carry an unmistakable smell. Two of Switzerland's most famous products – cheese and chocolate – are unthinkable without milk, and without cows dotting mountainsides Swiss tourism would not be the same.

About 40 000 different species of animals inhabit Switzerland, most of them insects, none of them really spectacular. But as an Alpine country, it boasts animals and plants not found on lower elevations, including the nimble chamois or the iconic edelweiss.

Despite being densely settled, still more than half of the country's territory is woodland or pristine nature. And the Swiss love nature: hiking is their favourite past-time. Carefully maintained trails have a total length of 62 416 km, long enough to reach one and a half times around the globe.

The Swiss have one of the world's strictest environmental and nature protection laws – and not just recently: in 1914 they created their first national park.

Wildlife

IBEX

Proud symbol of Canton Graubunden, it almost went extinct 200 years ago. All animals alive today are descendants of a few dozen ibex protected by the royal house of Savoy.

BIRDS

Around 400 different species of birds has been observed in Swiss airspace However, the exact number differs from one bird lover association to another.

FOXES

RED DEER

FISH

MARMOTS

They scurry all over the mountains, b they're concentrated in Zermatt (mor than 1000 animals). This town is to the what Punxsutawney is to Groundhog Phil. Every year around March 19, the leave their dens to announce spring.

BEARS

Cuddly and nice in Bern's bearpit opposite the old town. Considered a menace, when one or two stroll over from Italy, where they've been rescued from extinction. The good ones have names: Berna, Urs and Finn. The others go by numbers: M13 and JJ3.

LYNX

Driven out of Switzerland in 1894 (although one was spotted in 1909). Successful resettlement starting in 1971.

CHAMOIS

Famed for their sure-footedness in rocky terrain, but, unhappily for them, for their soft leather, too.

BATS

In Switzerland there are 30 known bat species.

SQUIRREL

HORSES

Along the Swiss-italian border, wild horses can be seen enjoying the views and pastures that Mt. Generoso offers.

WOLVES

Split the nation into those who fear Red Riding Hood Revisited and those who take a love of canines too far. The debate seems overblown, given that – having been driven out – only 40 wolves are known to roam the country. But they do kill sheep.

CHICKENS

Not wildlife, just food

HARVEST MOUSE

TICKS

Nasty little bloodsuckers that are now practically everywhere at elevations under 1500 meters. They cause up to 12 000 bouts of illness a year.

COWS

KUHSCHWEIZER (COW SWISS)

So close is the Swiss' relationship with their cows that snide Germans suspected it to be romantically inclined. They coined the invective **Kuhschweizer** (cow Swiss) which still succeeds in raising tempers.

LLAMAS

A recent addition to the Swiss countryside. The import from South America has proved to be highly effective to protect the declining sheep population against wolves. Apparently, they dislike being spat upon.

FLYING COWS

Pigs don't fly, but cows do. Every summer, Switzerland's air rescue service has to bring cattle to safety that have strayed off into inaccessible parts of the mountains.

BEAUTY CONTESTS

When men in Ancient Greece wanted to flatter women, they called them **cow-eyed**. A distant echo survives in beauty contests for cows all over Switzerland. The winner gets to wear a crown – like Miss Universe.

COW BELLS

Most cows wear one, allegedly to make sure you find the critters in case they get lost. Many bells are still handmade and tuned differently in order to create some bovine symphony on the pasture. Animal rights groups, however, worry that the bells damage the cows' hearing.

ALPINE PASTURE

Every summer, cows take a holiday in the mountains. Fresh air, fresh water, grass and herbs make for happy cattle and good milk. Farmers swear that cows look forward to their vacation.

ALPABFAHRT

Literally "driving down from mountain", this autumn event is Switzerland's answer to the Wild West: decorated with flowers and weighed down by big bells, cows make their way back to their stables. The **Alpabfahrt** in Appenzell draws thousands of visitors and is broadcast live on TV.

⩗ FIGHTS

No toreros are hurt in this event in canton Valais. Cows, the size of small mastodons, have it out in what is called the queenly fight: **combat des reines**. The winner is accorded the proud title **La Reine des reines** – queen of the queens.

COWS FOR RENT ⩗

Beset by low milk prices, more and more farmers resort to rent-a-cow schemes aimed at city dwellers. You may not take your cow home, though, just visit, pat or even milk her. On top of drinking milk direct from her udder, you may also purchase some of the priciest cheese you've ever bought.

For Rent

Flora

MEADOWS

Lush, vibrant and colourful, the meadows of our youth. For cows, they're a culinary feast, containing up to 50 different tasty species of plants per 100 m². Meadows are only mowed twice a year to maintain their diversity. As opposed to those veritable smorgasbords, fields provide the bovines' humdrum daily fare.

Switzerland has 3000 different native plants, nearly a third of which are flowers. Pretty and pleasing to the eye, some of their English names sound rather forbidding:

MOURNING WIDOW

Pretty, hairy leaves

ASTHMA WEED

Caution: contains an acrid, milky sap.

DEVIL'S PLAYTHING

Greek hero Achilles put it on his wounds

HAIRY CAT'S EAR

Edible in salads Or stir-fries

MONKEY-FLOWER

Salty and bitter taste.

TREES

Mess with them at your peril. Trimming or felling trees is a confounding legal maze. Take a lawyer along with your saw. One third of Switzerland is woodland, and the size of Switzerland's forest are growing by about 7000 football fields a year.

BEES

Must be paid princely fees after starring in the award-winning documentary **More than Honey**. How else to explain the steep price of honey in Switzerland? Acutely threatened by mites, every colony produces just a paltry eight kilos a year making a total of about 100 tons. In comparison: in neighbouring Austria it's 5000 tons.

There are about 350 invasive plant species in Switzerland, crowding out native flora.

FIVE-FACED BISHOP

Only smells in the evening.

ENZIAN

Edelweiss' bright blue brother, this alpine plant of the gentiana family is cherished for its medicinal properties, especially in herbal spirits and liqueurs. Angostura, Aperol and Underberg all contain it.

BLUE BUTCHER ORCHID

Found as far south as the Canary Islands and as far east as Iran.

ELWEISS

mbol of Alpine pride: it adorns an airline's livery, five Franc coin, patriotic shirts, and the insignia f the nation's highest military ranks – up to the four-edelweiss-general in times of war.

HEALTH

CONGRATULATIONS, MR. SCHMID.
YOUR TRANSPLANT WAS A TOTAL SUCCESS!!

I t is sometimes said that the Gotthard road tunnel is as clean as a hospital operating theatre. This is meant, of course, as a compliment to the tunnel, not a slur on Swiss clinics. They are pristinely immaculate – almost fit for a train.

In fact, you couldn't find a better place to fall ill than Switzerland, with 572 modern hospitals filled with state-of-the-art equipment and exceedingly well-trained doctors and nurses. Many of them, alas, are German, as college places for medicine at Swiss universities are still in woefully short supply.

Everyone residing in the country has to have health insurance. As they're all private and not state-run providers, they tend to be quite pricey. This, in turn, leads to a veritable smorgasbord of policy choices – utterly baffling to outsiders and newcomers – as the insured needs to choose which kind of doctors, illnesses, hospitals and body parts they want covered at an extra charge on top of a basic package.

Rarely included is dental care. Treatment is usually paid straight from patient to dentist. If need be, the former can always take out a mortgage to cover that new bridgework. Or go to Hungary.

Acute cost consciousness, however, has made Switzerland a pioneer in Europe for managed care and HMOs. Attempts to introduce a state health system along British or French lines have so far been rebuffed by voters.

Healthcare

BIRTH

The Swiss like babies, or babies like Switzerland: a record 86 000 children were born in 2015, continuing a decade-long baby boom. Mothers with an immigrant background contribute substantially to this high number.

INSURANCE

What does health have to do with a residence permit? Everything. Without a private Swiss health insurance, nobody is allowed to stay in the country officially.

PATIENTS

Swiss suffer – and die – from the same illnesses as people in other developed countries: chiefly cardiovascular diseases and cancer. Once, however, there was **"la maladie Suisse"**: homesickness. It was first diagnosed in Swiss mercenaries and treated as a physical affliction. Doctors assumed that it was triggered by thicker air in lower elevations.

INSURANCE

DOCTORS' SALARIES

CHF 200 000 per year on average – highest in Europe.

ABORTIONS

10 256 (2015) or about 1000 women – lowes Europe

HOSPITAL

HOSPITALS

With 5.5 beds per 1000 people, you're never far from a hospital – 70% of which are run by the cantons, the others are privately owned. Patients can chose freely from an approved list. Some private clinics can be quite costly, running at up to 3000 francs a night – before treatment. But they might include a Michelin-starred chef. Despite high prices, health tourism is booming: Switzerland is the 2nd largest market in Europe.

PEOPLE WITH DISABILITIES

Around one million people are registered as having a disability. The actual number could be much higher since glasses or hearing aides constitute an impairment, too.

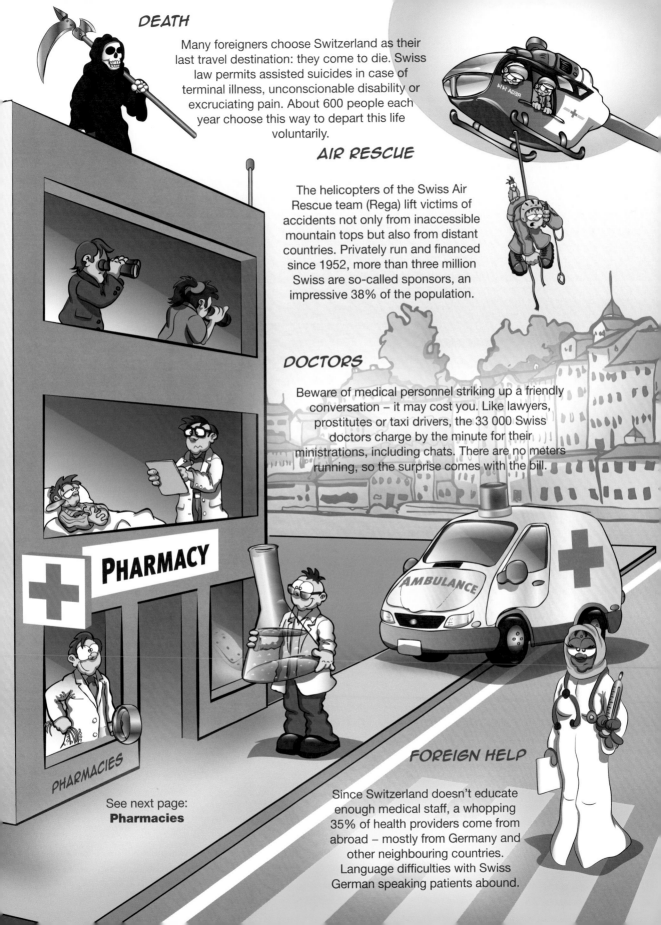

DEATH

Many foreigners choose Switzerland as their last travel destination: they come to die. Swiss law permits assisted suicides in case of terminal illness, unconscionable disability or excruciating pain. About 600 people each year choose this way to depart this life voluntarily.

AIR RESCUE

The helicopters of the Swiss Air Rescue team (Rega) lift victims of accidents not only from inaccessible mountain tops but also from distant countries. Privately run and financed since 1952, more than three million Swiss are so-called sponsors, an impressive 38% of the population.

DOCTORS

Beware of medical personnel striking up a friendly conversation – it may cost you. Like lawyers, prostitutes or taxi drivers, the 33 000 Swiss doctors charge by the minute for their ministrations, including chats. There are no meters running, so the surprise comes with the bill.

PHARMACY

PHARMACIES

See next page:
Pharmacies

AMBULANCE

FOREIGN HELP

Since Switzerland doesn't educate enough medical staff, a whopping 35% of health providers come from abroad – mostly from Germany and other neighbouring countries. Language difficulties with Swiss German speaking patients abound.

PHARMACIES

In any other country, one can go to a supermarket and buy an Aspirin, ibuprofen, eye drops, or any other over-the-counter medications. But not in Switzerland. Pharmacies control the handling of all medicines, making prices slightly higher, and the opportunity to self medicate somewhat lower.

LIFE EXPECTANCY

Good and healthy food, lots of sport and outdoor activity as well a high quality of life: the Swiss are a pretty fit, trim and contented lot. This is reflected in their life spans: men can expect to live until 81, women until 85.2 years of age – second only to Japan. The news is even better for those born after 1995. Their projected life-expectancy is 103.

DEFENCE & SAFETY

Peaceful, friendly, neutral, and home to both the Red Cross and the United Nations – Switzerland is a model nation, threatening no one and even helping others to defuse their tensions.

But appearances can be deceiving: just 30 years ago, the Swiss had one of Europe's largest standing armies, with additional reservists on 24 hours standby. "Switzerland doesn't have an army", it was said. "Switzerland is an army."

Today, while military service is still compulsory, the only astonishing facts about the armed forces are the speed and the extent of their demise: down from more than 500 000 to, eventually, only about 100 000 soldiers. The air force works 9 to 5 office hours, and voters turned down the purchase of new fighter planes.

But they did decide to keep the draft, though that was no foregone conclusion. Back in 1989, more than one third of voters wanted to abolish the armed forces altogether.

Historically, the Swiss were a feared and fierce military power. Even after they chose to stay out of international conflicts, they continued to hire out their farm boys as mercenaries to the highest bidder. These men were expensive, but cruel and effective. In other words: a Swiss quality product, worth every penny.

Today's last Swiss mercenaries protect the pope in Rome, but other nations must not eschew Swiss military hardware: with sales worth nearly half a billion dollars, the country's arms industry ranks eleventh in the world.

The Swiss Neutral Army

SWISS ARMY

Total strength 180 000 (incl. reserves) and shrinking. Eventually, no more than 100 000 are planned. Still less extreme than a plan pursued by a pacifist group to abolish the whole thing. Voters turned them down twice.

EQUIPMENT

To make sure reservists come prepared, they keep their assault rifle at home. However, this once much vaunted **Army in the wardrobe** has been lacking teeth lately: ammunition is only issued after arrival at the barracks.

PEACE SUPPORT

Around 300 soldiers are serving in peace support operations abroad.

Don't shoot! We're Neutral

STANDARD WEAPON

SG550

FOREIGN FORCES

Remaining neutral since 1515, Switzerland keeps its armed forces at home – with one exception. The Swiss Guard has protected popes for over 500 years. Applicants must be Swiss, Catholic, bachelors, and at least 174 cm tall. Given that Renaissance-style knee-breeches are part of the uniform, shapely calves are a plus, too.

IN CASE OF WAR

SHELTERS

A nation underground – and room to spare: Allegedly 114% of the Swiss population can find refuge in shelters big and small – car parks, hospitals or private homes. In peacetime, private shelters are used to store ski equipment and wine.

SWISS AIR FORCE

Just 56 aging Hornet and Tiger fighter planes, but a replacement was turned down by voters as too expensive. More embarrassing: The air force keeps office hours. Luckily, when a hijacked plane rudely headed for Geneva airport early in the morning in 2014, French fighter planes swooped in to help.

FORTIFICATIONS

Air bases and arms depots inside mountains, secret tunnels everywhere – Switzerland resembles an explosive Swiss cheese. Add fortifications and hidden gun emplacements as well as booby-trapped bridges and highways and you understand the image of the feisty hedgehog.

WOMEN IN ARMS

Women represent less than 1% of the total, however, more than half end up in leadership positions.

SWISS NAVY

Well, not really. But landlocked Switzerland shares watery borders with all its neighbours: lakes Constance, Geneva and Maggiore, plus the Rhine with Liechtenstein. The lakes are patrolled by fast craft – ten in all – which are armed with machine guns front and aft.

CONSCRIPTION

Mandatory for every male. Many dodge, others do civilian service. Boot camp is 18 to 21 weeks. But not so fast: up to age 30, three weeks of "refresher" training each year. The highest rank is lieutenant-general. A full general is only appointed in war-time.

PROFESSIONAL SOLDIERS

3400

MILITARY EXPENDITURE

Currently less than 1% of the GDP

CIVILIAN SERVICE

The 20th century was almost over before Switzerland offered a civilian alternative to military service, albeit only for conscientious objectors. Since 1992, young men have been able to choose from 1400 institutions in health, welfare, and environmental organisations as well as on farms or in museums. Overseas deployments are also possible.

Some 50 000 people each year take this option. Just to make sure they don't forget that they are shirking their duties to defend the nation, their service is one and a half times as long as the military version: 390 days instead of 260.

NEUTRALITY

*Some myths surround this much-vaunted concept, the most persistent being
that the Swiss abandoned fighting after their defeat by the French in the battle of
Marignano in 1515. In fact, they still loved a good fight – either with each other
or for some well-paying foreign client. The reason they stopped conquering new
territories was simpler: every new acquisition would have upset the delicate religious
balance between Protestant and Catholic cantons. Eventually, neutrality was forced
on them by the Congress of Vienna in 1815.*

*Major European powers didn't want any one of their rivals to make a grab at
the strategically important Alpine passes. So the lands around them had to be
neutralised. Being neutral has stood Switzerland in good stead, as it emerged from
other nations' wars in better shape than before.*

CONSCRIPTS ON TRAINS

It's a sight that can freeze your blood: a testosterone-driven young male in camouflage with an assault rifle slung over his shoulder taking the seat next to you on the train. Don't panic, it's just a conscript soldier going home from military service. Unlike soldiers in other countries, the Swiss don't leave their hardware behind at the barracks when they go and see mum. Always prepared – that's their motto.

SWISS ARMY KNIFE

The army's equipment – i.e. aging fighter planes – may not always be cutting-edge, but nothing cuts (or screws, bores, files, saws, writes, stores data, etc.) better than the Swiss Army Knife. Developed in the 1880s, it is still issued to every soldier. With annual sales of 26 million knives it's also a global success story largely thanks to American soldiers returning home with them after World War II. It even survived a 30% slump following the post-9/11 ban on pocket knives in planes. Originally, they were only handed out to officers, which probably explains the thoughtful inclusion of a corkscrew. Privates prefer beer to wine. The Swiss usually get their priorities right.

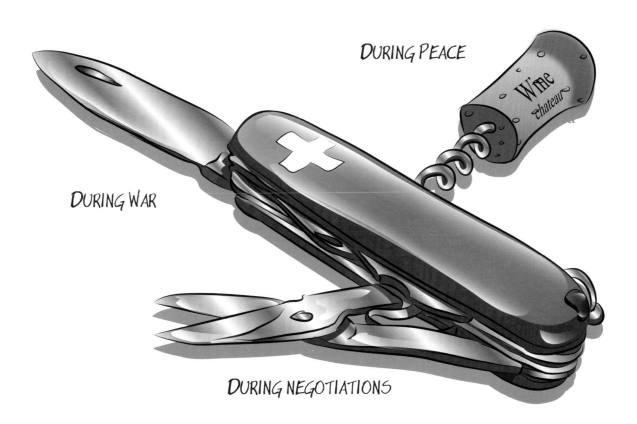

DURING PEACE

DURING WAR

DURING NEGOTIATIONS

FUNNY RULES

Forget "Look, mum, no hands" – just taking your feet off the pedals or riding a bike without a bell can result in a fine.

Want to move your parked car to a different spot? You have to "reinsert" it into moving traffic first. The space will be gone by the time you're back, but you saved yourself a CHF 40 fine.

No upright peeing after ten: persistent myth, invented by Boris Johnson when he was London's mayor. It's not true: you're free to urinate in your own home whenever the need arises – as long as you do it quietly. And postpone flushing until morning.

Peeing in public, however, is fraught with danger. In addition to causing a public nuisance, you're harming the dignity of the dandelion you're peeing on, as the constitution endows every creature with dignity, plants included. Maximum fine: 5 years in jail. Lamp posts or walls offer no escape. That will only lead to wilful damage to property.

Feel dirty at night? A quick shower after ten is permitted. Running a bath isn't according to rental contracts. Even Swiss sleep is protected by law. So, no music, no beating carpets, no hoovering, no high heels on wood floors, and no arguments, marital or otherwise. Just lie down and sleep.

You can leave your car by the roadside. You can leave it unlocked. But it'll cost you CHF 60 if you leave the keys inside. Car theft should not be encouraged or facilitated.

Holy Day: hanging up washing in public on Sundays is also not permitted in many properties. Why? Because it doesn't look nice. Good thing that running a washing machine is banned, too.

Never mind the washing. Flying a flag needs solid theoretical grounding. "Reglement 51.340" comprises 80 tightly spaced pages. This includes aesthetics: "Unbedecked poles next to bedecked poles look ugly."

FOOD & DRINK

No pizza, burger or sweet-and-sour pork – Switzerland's contribution to global cuisine is neither fast food nor finger food, as fondue requires lots of hardware on the table. On top of that, most Swiss recipes are not for the lactose intolerant.

All of this notwithstanding, Switzerland is anything but a culinary wasteland. The traditional cuisine may betray its rustic peasant origins – cheese, bread, potatoes, meat in modest bite-sized morsels only – but it has been refined to a high standard.

The country boasts an astonishing 116 Michelin-starred restaurants, of which three display the highest three star rating. Additionally, 72 eating establishments were awarded 19 of the maximum 20 points which Gault Millau, the other prestigious restaurant guide, bestows.

The best-known Swiss foods – leaving aside chocolate and muesli – are fondue and raclette, which are basically variations of melted cheese. Potatoes, the other peasant staple, are the main ingredient of Rösti, an elaborate form of roast potatoes which are often served with Zurcher Gschnetzeltes: thin slices of veal sautéed with butter, cream and white wine.

The Swiss love eating out, spending more than 20 billion francs a year at 26 000 eating establishments. They usually insist on quality, and this includes the wine, which very often comes from Swiss vineyards.

But foreigners beware: especially in rural areas, restaurants still stick to rigid feeding times. Lunch is served between 12.00 and 14.00 sharpish, dinner from 18.00 to half past nine. After all, people go to bed early.

Swiss Cuisine

BARBECUE

If it burns, you can drink[...] Russians say. If it sizzles, yo[...] grill it, the Swiss might a[...] Switzerland is one big barb[...] nation. In summer, the sce[...] fried meat hangs over the e[...] country.

VEGETARIANS

Can enjoy Swiss cuisine, too, with lots of fresh fruit and veg. Zurich boasts the world's oldest vegetarian restaurant. Hiltl's was founded in 1897 by a man who was a patient of müesli man Bircher-Brenner.

RACLETTE

Looks easy, but is actually quite complex. In other words: a very Swiss dish. You melt cheese on your own little pan. Then you garnish it to your liking.

ZÜRCHER GESCHNETZELTES

Twists your tongue when you pronounce it, loosens it when you eat it. Finely sliced strips of veal, Zurich's signature dish is cooked with white wine and cream. Rösti on the side.

Swiss key sec[...] ingredients

MÜESLI

The world's favourite breakfast dish started life as a dinner option, often in jails. In 1900, medical doctor Maximilian Oskar Bircher-Brenner soaked oatmeal in water, then added lemon juice, condensed milk, grated apples and nuts. Strangely enough, it caught on.

PAPRIKA

P

AROMAT

Oatmeal

HORSE MEAT

lso on the menu...

FONDUE

Miraculix, the druid but with cheese bubbling in his cauldron. No less fortifying than the magic potion on a cold winter night. Only tourists eat fondue in summer.

WHITE WINE

The best cheese fondue companion.

CATS

In some areas, cats are on the menu – provided it's not your neighbour's kitty.

ÖSTI

ese roast potatoes
as golden, warm and urishing as the disk of a ingtime sun. Crunchy side and soft within, the cret lies in the right potatoes.

ZOPF

The traditional must-have for Sunday's breakfast

BREAD

The Swiss love their bread, in any of their more than 200 traditional forms. Perhaps that's the reason why they experience great joy and pride baking their own bread and even giving it away as a gift (in particular Zopf). This is even more true when they find themselves living abroad.

CHESTNUTS

e a staple to help poor o peasants through the inter. Now they're a cacy for a sweet tooth: candied **maroons** cés or in **vermicelli**: ghetti-shaped, pureed estnuts that look like ms. Hence the name.

Drink

COFFEE

The Swiss company Nestlé twice revolutionized coffee-drinking. Their Nescafe brand – launched in 1938 – became synonymous for instant coffee. Revolution 2.0 is more recent: Nespresso coffee capsules. What else?

PANACHÉ

When it's really hot some find straight beer a bit too strong. Hence the solution called panaché or Panasch – half beer and half lemonade.

RIVELLA

Whey is the the unpalatable part of milk, which is why the Swiss turned it into a soda. First concocted in 1950, they drink 80 million of the 105 million litres produced annually. Clearly an acquired taste.

It has been illegal to smoke in bars and restaurants since 2010

WATER

From Adelbodener to Valser – Switzerland boasts more than 20 natural springs, producing more than 500 million litres per year. No need, though, to take to the (water) bottle: not only is tap water drinkable, but so too is water from many rivers and lakes.

WINE

The Romans brought vines to Helvetia. Today, virtually every canton produces reds and whites – 100 million litres per year. Almost all of it is consumed nationally.

MILK

One could fill a lake with the 3.5 million tons of milk siphoned from 550 000 udders every year. Most of it goes into cheese, yoghurt and butter, as the Swiss drink less milk: consumption is down to one small glass per person per day.

BEER

Almost five times more beer than wine is consumed – 480 million litres per year. The number of breweries has skyrocketed from 32 in 1990 to almost 500 today – mostly brewing bespoke craft beers, including one that mimics caipirinha.

ABSINTH

Once the muse of Baudelaire, Gauguin and Edgar Allan Poe, the vermouth drink from the Val de Travers was banned as dangerous for almost 100 years. Re-introduced in the late 1990s, the Green Fairy has made a remarkable comeback.

SPIRITS

Pfluemli, Kirsch or Williams pear – there's nary a fruit the Swiss won't distill into hooch. Some 50 distilleries produce 100 different kinds of spirits.

OVALTINE

Called Ovomaltine in German after the ingredients ovum (egg) and maltine (malts), the name got shortened due to a spelling mistake on the British patent application. Now drunk in more than 100 countries, it was developed in 1904 in Bern.

Chocolate

For a long time after its introduction in Europe, chocolate was an acquired taste: a crumbling grey powder, bitter as gall. Small wonder it was sold by apothecaries as expensive medicine.

INNOVATION

The Swiss changed everything – not so much for improving the taste but their earnings. They were the first to add sugar, milk and hazelnuts, because they wanted to save on expensive cocoa beans.

PRODUCTION

181 414 tons per year, worth 1.7 bn francs. More than half is exported.

There are 18 major chocolate producers and numerous smaller manufacturers.

SWISS CHOCOLATE PIONEERS

Francois-Louis Cailler (1796–1852) created the chocolate bar.

Philippe Suchard (1797–1884) added sugar to cocoa powder.

Charles-Amédée Kohler (1790–1874) supplemented cocoa beans with hazelnuts.

Daniel Peter (1836–1919) diluted the mixture with cheap milk.

Rodolphe Lindt (1855–1909) enabled the gold bunny with his conching method.

Theodore Tobler (1876–1941) added nougat and honey to his Matterhorn-shaped Toblerone.

WATCHDOGS ON THE PROWL

Trade body **Chocosuisse** is constantly on alert to track down false Swiss chocolate produced abroad.

THE MASTERMIND

Chocolate's inadvertent genius was **Rodolphe Lindt.** One Friday evening, he forgot to turn off a mixer he'd developed (called a **conche**). The unexpected 78 hours of stirring created chocolate as we know it: soft, sweet and melting in the mouth.

PRESENTATION

Matterhorn look alikes, golden bunnies and teddies, pralines and truffle balls – everything seems to be turned into chocolate. But the plain chocolate bar tops the list with 48 percent of all choco products.

SWEET TEETH

The world was eternally grateful and today buys more than 100 000 tons of Swiss chocolate per year. The Swiss themselves are their own best customers – with every single one consuming 10 kilograms a year.

Cheese

French president Charles de Gaulle famously complained about the difficulty of governing a country with 246 different kinds of cheese. Luckily, Swiss citizens govern themselves. Otherwise, there's no way of knowing what would happen – with approximately 450 cheeses of all sorts. A cheesy fault line runs between French and German speaking cantons, with Romands specializing in bries, while their German speaking compatriots prefer harder fare.

GRUYÈRE

Made from the milk of gourmet cows. They get only the best grass and wholesome herbs.

MOZZARE

Believe it or not, the number one cheese in Switzerland is mozzarella. The Swiss eat more than 400 tons per year. 80% of this produced in Switzerland.

VACHERIN

Sinfully seductive, the creamy and warm Mont d'Or rests in a pine box, ready to be spooned out. Bliss.

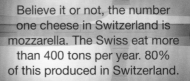

APPENZELLER

TÊTE DE MOINE

The herb-rich grass in Alpine meadows gives it a tangy flavour. During ripening, it's rubbed with a top-secret herbal brine.

SCHABZIGER

Literally monk's head, first produced 800 years ago in Bellelay Abbey in canton Jura. Shaped like little rosettes.

The nation's earliest cheese from canton Glarus. It became Switzerland's first international brand name. Very hard and grated like parmesan.

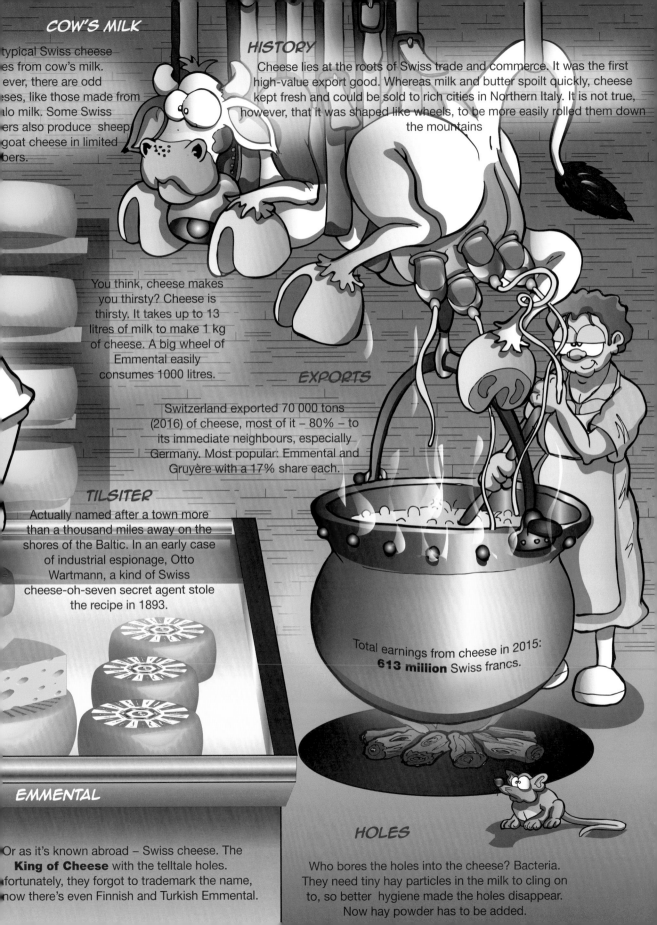

COW'S MILK

typical Swiss cheese
es from cow's milk.
ever, there are odd
eses, like those made from
alo milk. Some Swiss
ers also produce sheep
goat cheese in limited
bers.

HISTORY

Cheese lies at the roots of Swiss trade and commerce. It was the first high-value export good. Whereas milk and butter spoilt quickly, cheese kept fresh and could be sold to rich cities in Northern Italy. It is not true, however, that it was shaped like wheels, to be more easily rolled them down the mountains

You think, cheese makes you thirsty? Cheese is thirsty. It takes up to 13 litres of milk to make 1 kg of cheese. A big wheel of Emmental easily consumes 1000 litres.

EXPORTS

Switzerland exported 70 000 tons (2016) of cheese, most of it – 80% – to its immediate neighbours, especially Germany. Most popular: Emmental and Gruyère with a 17% share each.

TILSITER

Actually named after a town more than a thousand miles away on the shores of the Baltic. In an early case of industrial espionage, Otto Wartmann, a kind of Swiss cheese-oh-seven secret agent stole the recipe in 1893.

Total earnings from cheese in 2015: **613 million** Swiss francs.

EMMENTAL

Or as it's known abroad – Swiss cheese. The **King of Cheese** with the telltale holes. fortunately, they forgot to trademark the name, now there's even Finnish and Turkish Emmental.

HOLES

Who bores the holes into the cheese? Bacteria. They need tiny hay particles in the milk to cling on to, so better hygiene made the holes disappear. Now hay powder has to be added.

SPORTS

What determines a nation's sporting prowess? The number of Olympic medals? Or the people's state of health and fitness?

Switzerland does fairly well in both. Since the beginning of the modern Olympic Games in 1896, Swiss sportsmen and women have won 323 gold, silver and bronze medals at summer and winter games. Not bad for a small country of just eight million people.

They're definitely not a nation of couch potatoes who just watch their heroes like tennis star Roger Federer on TV. More than two-thirds of Swiss engage at least once a week in some kind of physical exercise.

Topping the list is hiking, the national pastime, followed by biking, swimming and skiing. Added to that are some special and, frankly, weird Swiss sports like Schwingen or Hornussen.

Incidentally, the number of bikers and skiers in the country is roughly the same: about three million. It is possible that these are the same people alternating between snow and asphalt.

It used to be said that Swiss kids knew how to ski before they could walk. Today, the same is true for their ability to pedal a bike before they take their first baby steps.

All that training seems to have an effect. Compared to their European neighbours (let alone Americans), the Swiss are a fairly well-toned lot. They die old – at 82.8 on average – and slim: almost 60 percent of the population has a healthy or lower-than-normal BMI.

Summer Sports

From American football to water polo – there's hardly a sport that cannot be practiced in Switzerland. People are organized in more than 20 000 sport clubs.

CYCLING

Hundreds of special national, regional and local routes. Bikes can be rented at railway stations. For those who don't like pedalling: it is downhill all the way from the Gotthard to Bellinzona.

STEINSTOSSEN

Probably the oldest national sport, this stone toss was probably played in prehistoric times. Today, the Unspunnenstein is thrown. At 83.5 kg, it is the motherlode of the traditional stone toss. The current record sits at 4.11 metres

TENNIS

Irrevocably linked to the most famous Swiss – Roger Federer. He, Martina Hingis and Stan Wawrinka make Switzerland a world power in at least one sport.

ORIENTEERING

Anyone can run 100 metres without getting lost, and even marathon routes are demarcated. Orienteering means dashing through unfamiliar terrain, navigating with map and compass. The Swiss are really good at it, with 94 gold, silver and bronze medals.

First used in 1808 and stolen twice by separatists from the Jura mountains, its replica is now stored in a bank vault alongside other – and smaller –precious stones.

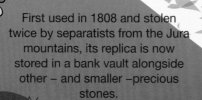

FOOTBALL

Popular mainly as a spectator sport, with fans often supporting teams from neighbouring countries. Some Swiss clubs' names hark back to the sport's English roots: Young Boys Bern and Grasshoppers Zurich.

SCHWINGEN

Alpine wrestling, performed in pits of sawdust by men – and lately women – of impressive stature. The national champion is Schwinger König – the only king in republican Switzerland.

MOUNTAIN BIKING

The longest trail is 665 kilometres between Scuol in the East to Aigle at the French border.

JASS

A more sedentary sport, it's Switzerland's defining card game. A progenitor of American pinochle, it is largely inscrutable to outsiders. It can also be mind-numbingly dull when Swiss state TV broadcasts hours-long games live.

HORNUSSEN

Fancy stopping a bullet with a flimsy wooden shingle? That's what's required in Hornussen, a traditional game which looks like a cross of misunderstood golf and baseball. The puck, called a **Nouss** is hit with a 3 m long whiplike stick and reaches 300 km/h.

Winter Sports

The British invented winter sports 150 years ago. Lacking their own proper mountains, they picked unsuspecting Switzerland for their new-fangled pastime. The Swiss have been saying "merci" ever since.

Number of **snow canons**: more than 16 000.

Climate change and lack of snow threaten destinations below 1000 metres.

7400 km of ski pistes

SKIING

As a rule, Swiss ignore their Austrian neighbours. That changes in international skiing competitions. Sadly, the Austrians often win.

SKATING

Most people prefer lakes to rinks. Suvretta House hotel in St. Moritz offers the most perfectly polished, stylish surface.

WARNING

Death by **avalanche**: 23 per year on average.

CROSS-COUNTRY SKIING

Dario Cologna is a three-time Olympic gold medallist and world champion. Circumventing steep slopes, there are 5500 km of tracks.

TOBOGGANING

Europe's longest run near Grindelwald: **15 kilometres.**

620 km of toboggan runs

Number of toboggan accidents in Switzerland every year: around **12 000.**

SNOWBOARDING

Laax was the first resort to specially cater to hip, young snowboarders. Switzerland's snowboard world champion and Olympic gold medallist Iouri Podladtchikov trains here.

SKI PASS

Zermatt sells Europe's most expensive at CHF 79 per day.

CURLING

In summer, they throw a rock, in winter they propel it over ice. With one Olympic gold, five world and 11 European titles, Switzerland is number three in the world.

AMBRI PIOTTA

ix of Italian opera and ek tragedy: tucked away South of the Gotthard, ice hockey club is poor, indomitable. It has the dest stadium and the most loyal ns. Never won the Cup but weren't ever elegated, either.

ICE HOCKEY

First played almost 100 years ago, Spengler Cup in Davos is the world's oldest international ice hockey tournament.

POLITICS

As a rule, the Swiss like to keep things simple. That includes their political system. You see, in Switzerland, they take democracy literally: the people rule. That's what the Greek word means.

Consequently, Swiss voters have the last – and very often also the first – word in decisions. Many laws passed by parliament need to be signed off by the people. In addition, they can initiate laws.

Some pretend that this democratic paradise has existed since 1291 when the original Confederation was set up. Not quite. Inequalities and injustices persisted for centuries, and universal suffrage was – shamefully – only established in 1971 when women finally got the vote.

Women in politics apparently was no simple matter for male voters, but keeping things simple in general allows the Swiss to discard things that elsewhere would be considered indispensable for a functional state.

There is no prime minister. The powerless president officiates for just one year. The government includes all major parties, so ministers are forced to compromise. Strictly speaking, Switzerland doesn't even have a capital. Bern is just a convenience, called a federal city. Foreign states need a place for their embassies, after all.

Most importantly, the Swiss have jettisoned ideology. They know that all politics boil down to money: how much? Who pays? Do I need it?

Therefore, voters not only decide where their tax francs go. They determine their tax rates, too. And they've been known to raise them. It is at this point that outsiders totally fail to understand how the Swiss system works.

Government

Two chambers, based on the American model of House and Senate: The **National Council** and the **Council of States**.

The seats are currently divided among 12 different political parties.

EXECUTIVE BRANCH

Ever since its introduction in 1848, the **Federal Council** has consisted of only seven ministers. Traditionally, the four largest parties have one or two ministers in the cabinet. This forces the government to find compromise solutions. Opposing opinions are put forward by the voters.

LEGISLATIVE BRANCH

The 200 members of the National Council (**Nationalrat**) are elected according to the size of the constituencies. Small cantons send just one parliamentarian, mighty Zurich has 20.

CVRIA CONFOEDERATIONIS

FEDERAL CHANCELLO

The chancellor has no vote in the counc but communicates wit Federal Assembly

HEAD OF STATE

see next page: **The President**

COUNCIL OF STATES

Cantons are represented in the Council of States (**Ständerat**) with two members each, regardless of size. Exceptions are the six smallest cantons (Obwalden, Nidwalden, Basel-Stadt, Basel-Landschaft, Appenzell Innerrhoden, Appenzell Ausserrhoden) which only elect one councillor. All laws have to be passed by both chambers to come into force.

46 Members representing the cantons

FEDERAL ASSEMBLY

Both chambers make up the **United Federal Assembly**. It elects the government, the Federal Chancellor (head of the administration), federal judges and – in times of war – a general.

MILITIA SYSTEM

Misleading term for a simple principle: Swiss still prefer laymen to professionals in politics. Since pàrliàment generally convenes just four times a year for periods of three weeks at a time, this gives members the time to continue running their farm, business or law firm.

JUSTICE

There are four high courts: the **Federal Court**, the **Federal Criminal Court**, the **Federal Administrative Court** and **Federal Patents Court** – dealing each with respective types of cases. However, Switzerland does not have a constitutional court, as the people are considered the supreme and only arbiter on constitutional questions.

THE PRESIDENT

The ministers take turns being president of the confederation for one year.

Their job: they chair cabinet meetings and represent the country abroad. There is no prime minister or other head of government.

WEIBEL

Clad in their impressive early 19th century uniforms with cape and bicorn, they are a minister's personal aide and factotum.

LANDSGEMEINDE

*It may sound like folklore but it's serious, nitty-gritty politics: two cantons – Appenzell-Innerrhoden and Glarus – retain the ancient institution of the **Landsgemeinde**.*

Once a year, all eligible voters assemble in the main square of the canton's capital to discuss, debate and vote on political measures that have been prepared by parliament in the preceding 12 months. Voters can introduce new laws on the spot, too. Voting is done by show of hands or voting cards, and decisions taken by estimation of majority.

...THIRTEEN, FOURTEEN, FIFTEEN, SIXTEEN.....

Federalism

Every single village flies three flags in its main square: its own, the canton's and the federal Swiss cross. This reflects the trinity of Swiss federalism. All three components have their own rights and duties. The basic principle: decisions should be taken at the lowest possible level – closest to, and by, the people affected by them.

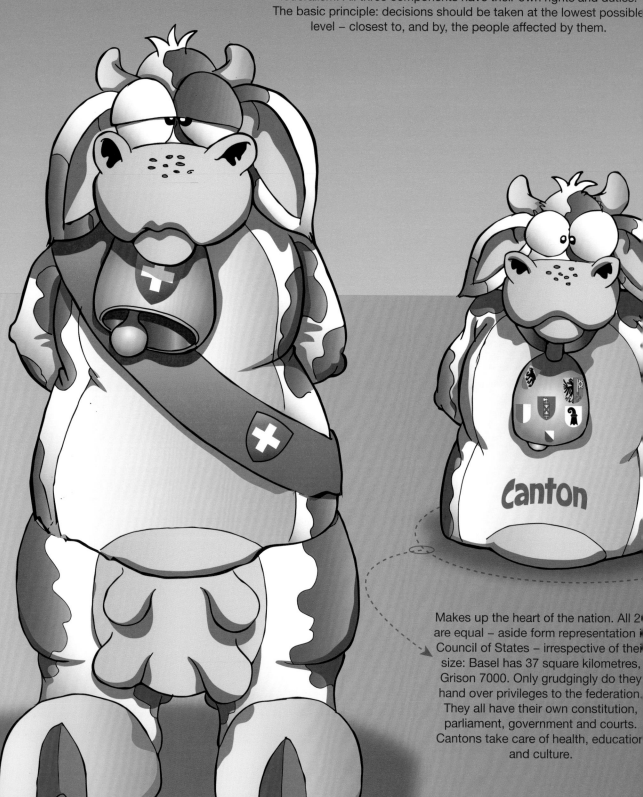

Canton

Makes up the heart of the nation. All 2[ ] are equal – aside form representation [ ] Council of States – irrespective of thei[r] size: Basel has 37 square kilometres, [ ] Grison 7000. Only grudgingly do they hand over privileges to the federation. They all have their own constitution, parliament, government and courts. Cantons take care of health, education and culture.

The body of the nation. Seen by many as a necessary evil. It took many attempts before Bern could raise federal taxes. The federation is in charge of foreign and defence policy as well as customs and fiscal matters. The money is printed by the national bank.

Federation

1

Commune

3

The soul of the nation. There are 2294, from Corippo, the smallest with 13 inhabitants to mighty Zurich with 416 000. The bigger ones have elected parliaments, but 80 per cent decide matters by convening all eligible citizens. They vote on affairs of schooling, welfare, energy supply, road building and – most importantly – taxes.

Law Making – Swiss style

PROPOSING A LAW

The vast majority of laws are initiated, discussed and passed by parliament. After all, its members are, just as in any other democracy, literally law-makers. The government, a political party, or any deputy can propose a law.

Everyone remotely concerned by the law is invited to discuss it: business groups, associations, lobbies, consumer groups.

REFERENDUM

Some acts of parliament ha to be voted on by voters, example anything that chang the constitution or internatio treaties. These are **obligato referenda**. The same syste applies to laws passed individual canto

Here comes the first Swiss speciality: if anyone – a political party, an interest group or even a single citizen – objects to a law, they can demand a referendum. If they collect **50 000 signatures** within **100 days**, the matter is put before the people to decide. A simple majority of voters can pass or sink the law. These are called **facultative referenda**.

GENERAL DEBATE OF A LAW

For this process the Swiss have a forbidding word:
Vernehmlassung
(consultative process)

VOTE IN PARLIAMENT

After both chambers have debated the proposed law, it is put to a vote. If the two chambers disagree, a compromise solution has to be worked out. So far, so good, so normal. This is how it works in most democratic countries.

INITIATIVE

This is where Swiss democracy gets exciting. Anyone can introduce **popular initiatives** – outside and even against parliament – provided they collect **100 000 signatures** in **18 months** to support their cause. After the matter has been discussed at length the initiative will be put before the people. Sometimes the government puts forward an alternative proposal. A double majority – of voters and cantons – is necessary for passage of a popular initiative that results in a change to the constitution.

THE VOTING MARATHON

No matter is too mundane or too momentous – it will be voted on by the Swiss electorate. They rule if dogs should be kept on a leash or if the country joins the United Nations. They decide if new fighter planes are to be bought, how tax on spirits should be distributed, or if they want to work fewer hours. "No", has always been the answer to the last question.

The right to approve legislation goes back to 1848 and 1874. The people's privilege to initiate legislation was enshrined in 1891. It can be argued, however, that people's power began in the 1270s, when all adult males of a community gathered to decide political questions.

Votes are held four times each year – in communities, cantons and on the federal level. The dates are set long in advance. Mark your agendas: on June, 3rd 2035 you'll be asked to vote – the topic yet to be decided.

THE POLITICS OF "CHANGE"

"Change" as a political slogan may resonate well with Americans. Swiss are not so sure. Even though they have the right to shake everything up, they very rarely do. Of 206 initiatives since 1891, only 18 have been adopted – most of them in the last 20 years.

World politics in CH

Switzerland is home to 25 international organisations and 250 NGOs which cover weather, trade, plants, diseases, railways and airlines. The choice was obvious: a clement meteorological and fiscal climate, good train and plane connections, and above all neutral ground.

When world football moved from Paris to Zurich in 1932, it was broke, had a bad reputation and a 300 square feet office. 75 years on, FIFA's reputation is even wors but it has cash reserves of $ 1.4 billion and a glass palace overlooking the town.

INTERNATIONAL ORGANISATION FOR MIGRATION

FIFA

INTERNATIONAL TELECOMMUNICATIONS UNION

INTERNATIONAL LABOR ORGANISATION

Founded in 1930 to facilitate Germany's WW I reparations. Today, the world's most powerful central bankers meet regularly on the top floor of the BIS's round office tower next to Basel railway station for dinner, discussions and decisions about the global economy.

Prior to its establishment in 1874, sending a letter internationally was tricky. For starters: who got the money for the stamp – the country where the letter was posted, or the country that delivered it? Based in Bern, the UPU still coordinates all (non-electronic) international mail.

BANK FOR INTERNATIONAL SETTLEMENTS

UNIVERSAL POSTAL UNION

INTER-PARLIAMENTARY UNION

Established in 1950 to stem Europe's post-WW II refugee crisis, the United Nation's High Commissioner for Refugees soon saw his agenda encompassing the whole world. There's still no end in sight for the plight of many millions of displaced people.

With more than 8000 meetings and conferences every year, Geneva is the UN's second most important seat after New York. The offices are housed in the Palais des Nations, a 1930s neoclassical building of fading charm and crumbling mortar that used to be the HQ of the League of Nations.

UNHCR

CROSSBOW SHOOTING UNION

UNITED NATIONS

Swiss businessman Jean Henri Dunant witnessed the carnage at the battle of Solferino in 1859 where 40 000 soldiers were killed or maimed. Deeply shaken, he founded the Red Cross as a neutral humanitarian body in wars. The emblem is said to be a colour reversal of the white cross on the Swiss flag.

FIFA's European sister was founded in 1954 in Basel before it eventually settled in Nyon near Geneva. Some sovereign nations are not members, like the Vatican. Some non-sovereign territories are, like the Faroe Islands. Sheep before clergy.

One of the UN's more important organisations, it was founded in Geneva in 1946 – incidentally with the help of US diplomat Alger Hiss, who was later sentenced as a Soviet spy.

BROKEN CHAIR

INTERNATIONAL FEDERATION OF SPORTS CHIROPRACTIC

UEFA

WORLD HEALTH ORGANISATION

Most photographed site after the Jet d'Eau, this 12-metre high sculpture of a wooden chair with one broken leg was erected in 1997 to protest land-mines.

WORLD BRIDGE FEDERATION

INTERNATIONAL ICE HOCKEY FEDERATION

WORLD ANTI-DOPING AGENCY

INTERNATIONAL BOXING ASSOCIATION

INTERNATIONAL BASEBALL FEDERATION

UNION CYCLISTE INTERNATIONALE

INTERNATIONAL OLYMPIC COMMITTEE

WORLD INTELLECTUAL PROPERTY ORGANISATION

Frenchman Pierre de Coubertin founded it in 1894 in Paris but relocated to neutral Lausanne in 1915. The IOC set a trend: Today, 27 international sport organisations are based in Switzerland – from the International Baseball Federation to the Crossbow Shooting Union.

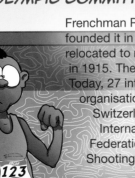

INTERNATIONAL AIR TRANSPORT ASSOCIATION

ECONOMY

When it comes to economic clout, the Swiss seem to think that size doesn't matter. How else could a country that ranks 134th in terms of area end up as number nine in per capita economic output? The Swiss constitute one tenth of a per cent of the world's population, but contribute one full per cent to global GDP – a whopping 685 billion dollars, 82 200 dollars per capita.

How do they do it? Do they work 24/7? Do they float on an ocean of crude or sit astride a mountain of rare elements? It can't be all cheese, clocks and chocolate.

In fact, Switzerland is bare of any natural resources. Trade was hampered domestically by forbidding mountains, internationally by the absence of coastlines and harbours.

If they wanted to make money, the Swiss had to use their prime resources: their wit, their business sense, their inventiveness, their thrift and an improbable sense of risk. Oh, and banking secrecy might have helped, too.

The result is one big throbbing economic powerhouse: the world's largest nutrition company (Nestlé), two of the biggest pharmaceutical firms (Roche and Novartis), leading banks (UBS and Credit Suisse), five of the top ten global commodities traders (Vitol, Gunvor, Glencore, Trafigura, Mercuria), insurers (Swiss Re), technology (ABB), even the most stylish manufacturer of toilets (Geberit, inventor of the flushing cistern) – they're all Swiss.

And yes, of course there's also Rolex watches, Lindor pralines, Akris fashion and Ricola herbal candy, too.

Commerce

LABOR FORCE

More than half of all Swiss are employed: 4.7 m
One third are foreigners, and the unemploymen
hasn't been above 5% since 1997.

99%
of Swiss
companies have
fewer than
250 employees.

MS Chuchichäschtli

SERVICES

Services constitute 72%
of the economy,

INNOVATION

Every year Switzerland spends close to
3% of its GDP, around CHF 19bn, on
research and development. Over
three-quarters of this funding comes from
the private sector.

TOURISM

Generates around the 6% of
GDP and employs about 4% of
the working population

TRADING
PARTNERS

Germany in first place for
exports (37bn francs) and
imports (47bn). Number two in
exports is the US (27bn), in
imports Italy (16bn). Third place
in both categories goes to
France (14bn exports, 13bn
imports)

DO YOU KNOW WERE I CAN FIND
THE NEAREST OCEAN?

MERCHANT NAVY

Landlocked they may be, but the Swiss have
a nifty little merchant navy of 49 ships with a
capacity of one million GRT. In 1943, the
Swiss freighter "Maloja" was accidentally
sunk by the RAF off Corsica.

GDP

A whopping CHF 642bn (80 200 per capita). Exports contribute 31.6% to GDP.

AGRICULTURE

Despite the bucolic postcard image, agriculture only contributes 1.2%.

Although the sector as a whole is declining, organic farming is steadily increasing: 11% of farms are now organic.

TRADE

ealthy balance with 203bn francs worth of exports and 6bn in imports. The Swiss mainly sell chemicals and armaceuticals (41.7%), precision instruments and tches (23%) and machinery (15.3%). They buy energy, hicles and consumer goods abroad.

CHEMICAL AND PHARMACEUTICAL

Switzerland's biggest export business employs 65 000 people at home and an additional 355 000 abroad.

INDUSTRY

Industry constitutes 26.8% of the economy.

RETAILERS

Migros and Coop are the two main retailers in Switzerland capturing 70% of the market. Together they employ 160 000.

VAT

witzerland's VAT s the lowest in Europe: 8% on most goods.

POVERTY AND WEALTH

You want to appear rich? Easy, just get a Swiss address or better still, a Swiss bank account. The idea that Swiss equals money is well founded: they are the richest people on earth. On average, every adult owns CHF 562 000. According to Credit Suisse's Global Wealth Report, that's almost twice the wealth of the second-placed Australians and eleven times the world average.

But this shiny coin has a dark side, too: more than half a million people – 6.6 percent – live in poverty. An additional one million are in acute danger of dropping below the poverty line.

SWISS MADE?

Domestic production costs are high, so Swiss companies manufacture abroad. This threatens the coveted Swissmade label – which is worth CHF 6bn a year to the economy. Now, at least 60% of production costs and most of the production process have to be local to qualify as truly Swiss.

FOREIGN COMPETITION

When German retail giants Aldi and Lidl invaded Switzerland some years ago, local supermarket chains Migros and Coop were stunned. But there was no law, tax or tariff with which they could stop them – except being better. It's Switzerland's preferred, and only method to fend off foreign competition.

SWISS MONEY

BANKS

As synonymous to Switzerland as watches, cheese and chocolate, but with a shadier reputation. Tax dodgers, tyrants' hidden nest-eggs, and a slew of financial tricksters saw to that. Still, the financial sector is vital to the country: It generates 13% of GDP, provides 6% of all jobs and pays 14% of all taxes. One-third of all global offshore funds are held in Switzerland.

SWISS FRANC NEW SERIES (NO.9)

Ambitious safety features and technical glitches delayed the latest series' issuance by – very un-Swiss – six years. For the first time, the central bank bade farewell to depicting famous Swiss on the notes. Instead, they'll show mountains, butterflies and ice crystals.

Les billets de banque sont protegés par le droit pénal.

Le banconote sono protette dal dititto penale.

BANQUE NATIONALE SUISSE
BANCA NAZIONALE SVIZZERA

Cinqua
Cinquar

44AK04051972

GOLD

Gold is barely found in Switzerland, but the country processes and trades 70% of the world's gold production.

The Swiss National Bank has the exclusive rights to issue Swiss Franc banknotes

SNB

OLD CHF 50

CURRENCY

The Swiss Franc is divided into 100 centimes. Introduced in 1798 by the French, the **Franc de Suisse** replaced cantonal currencies. Notes range from ten to 1000 francs. Every successive value is 11 mm longer than the preceding one. It's also the world's safest currency with no less than 18 security features.

Fünfzig Franken
Tschunchanta Francs

INTERNATIONAL

The Swiss franc is highly welcome all over the globe, but in the independent principality of Liechtenstein it's actually legal tender. Germans and Italians in the enclaves of Büsingen and Campione use the franc in everyday transactions, too.

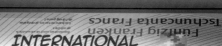

WAGES

Astonishingly high, but so is the cost of living. There's no general minimum wage, but CHF 4000 per month is considered a low wage.

TRANSPARENCY

New catchword, now that the venerable (some would say venal) law on banking secrecy has gone. Swiss bankers, once derided as the greedy gnomes of Zurich, now promise to be the cleanest of all the world's financial wizards.

NEW CHF 50
(2016)

SAVINGS

The Swiss are a thrifty nation: almost a quarter of their income (23%) is squirreled away in savings accounts, pension schemes or gold and cash in safe deposit boxes or under the mattress. Extensive loans and high levels of debt are still frowned upon.

...tzerland's biggest banks:
UBS
Credit Suisse
Raiffeisen
...rcher Kantonalbank

1000

Jacob Burckhardt 1818-1897

1000

Tausend Franken
Milli Francs

SNB   SNB

SCHWEIZERISCHE NATIONALBANK
BANCA NAZIUNALA SVIZRA

1000-FRANC-NOTE

The world's highest denomination banknote – compared to EUR 500, USD 100 and GBP 50. One million francs in 1000's is a pile just three inches high.

COINS

While banknotes proudly display modern design, coins have hardly changed since 1850. The 10-centimes-coin of 1879 is still in circulation. One major change: Lady Helvetia, once shown seated, is now standing up.

FINANCIAL NEUTRALITY

How to protect your wealth during an economic crisis? Buy gold, real estate or rare vintages? Yes, all of that – and best if you do it in Switzerland. The country has always been a safe haven of first and last resort in an emergency. During the 2008 financial crisis, foreign capital inflow spiked like a hypertensive patient's cardiogram, and the Swiss franc jumped to it's highest value ever in 2011.

Wars, revolutions, political upheavals – these are alien concepts to the Swiss. Unless they happen elsewhere, and Switzerland throws open its borders to frightened foreign currencies: dollars, euros, pounds get converted into stable francs.

PEOPLE

Libya's ex-dictator Muammar Gaddafi once made a suggestion that seemed – at least to him – eminently sensible: divide Switzerland and hand over the German, French and Italian parts to its larger neighbours. No one, he argued, would miss the country.

Well, at least the Swiss would. For while it is true that there's not much love lost between the Genevois, the Zürcher and the Southern Luganese, this hodgepodge of languages, religions, cultures, histories and wildly different cheeses does feel like one nation.

The key word is "Willensnation": a nation willed together by everybody's desire to be Swiss. Most Swiss, however, would be hard put to define what that Swissness entails. They'd probably name self-rule, direct democracy, self-reliance and a love for grilled sausages – solid, sober features, not grand and lofty notions of race and glory.

Right from the beginning, Switzerland was settled by diverse peoples: the Helvetians, dreamy but feisty Celts, who gave Caesar a run for his money. Later, the Alemanni trickled in – a flinty, tough Germanic tribe. Later still, Burgundian settlers in the West introduced French. South of the Alps, Latin merged into Italian.

Swiss Germans are dominant. There are 4.5 million (64%), as opposed to 1.7 million French-speakers (20%), 350 000 Italo-Swiss (9%), and the tiny group of 40 000 Rhaetians (0.5%).

Switzerland is still an immigrant nation: nearly a quarter of the population wasn't born here or doesn't hold a Swiss passport. Most feel thoroughly Swiss, though. Because it's their will.

Who are the Swiss?

There'll never be an answer, not even in this book. Like other nations, the Swiss are pretty diverse. Mind you, there are things that could be considered "typical". But then you'll find punctual, reliable and slightly boring Greeks, too.

The Swiss are proud of being Swiss, of running a well functioning and prosperous community all by themselves. Just as important, on the other hand, is their pride in being different from other Swiss – by birth, language, customs and occasionally even still religion.

Their big cities – young, modern, fast and mostly governed by left-wing or green party administrations – are on a different planet from the central valleys where churches and local notables still exert influence. But all are united when they shop at Migros, fly Swiss to their holiday destination, and vote in national referenda and elections.

And the country is changing. Only 30 years ago, Swiss society was more white, more male, more conservative. Men in suits with cigarettes between their lips ran banks, politics and the army – with revolving doors linking these institutions. Women stayed at home, cooking stodgy meals and raising well-behaved kids. Hell, they only got the right to vote in 1971.

Switzerland is different today, with the biggest difference being the arrival of foreigners. They brought their food, their customs and their language – but only up to a point. No matter what colour their skin, their children will enjoy fondue, go skiing and speak fluent Swiss German. Women, too, have altered the country. They have made it less harsh and obstinate.

HOW TO BECOME SWISS

It may no longer be the world's most coveted passport (this honour goes to Germany), but it is definitely one of the most difficult to acquire. Only after 12 years of uninterrupted residence – much of it in one place – you may hand in your application, which can take another couple of years to process. Commune, canton and confederation all have to approve, with the most difficult hurdles lurking at the lowest level: in some communities, would-be citizens have to pass muster with a majority of all citizens, who take a vote. Becoming Swiss doesn't come cheap, either: depending on income and place of residence, prepare to pay several thousand francs for your red book. Some relief is in sight, though: as of January 1, 2018, ten years of residence will be sufficient.

TAKE IT EASY

TO WORK OR NOT TO WORK...
THAT IS THE QUESTION

Americans, they say, work hard, not smart. With the Swiss it's the other way round: they accomplish a lot without short-changing their leisure time. They're just extremely flexible. They work from home, past retirement age, and one third of them reduce their workload to less than full-time to suit their needs or balance jobs with raising kids. Only the Dutch choose part-time work more often.

Foreign DNA

Switzerland always offered exile to political dissidents – irrespective of their opinions – provided, they didn't pursue their revolutionary interests here.

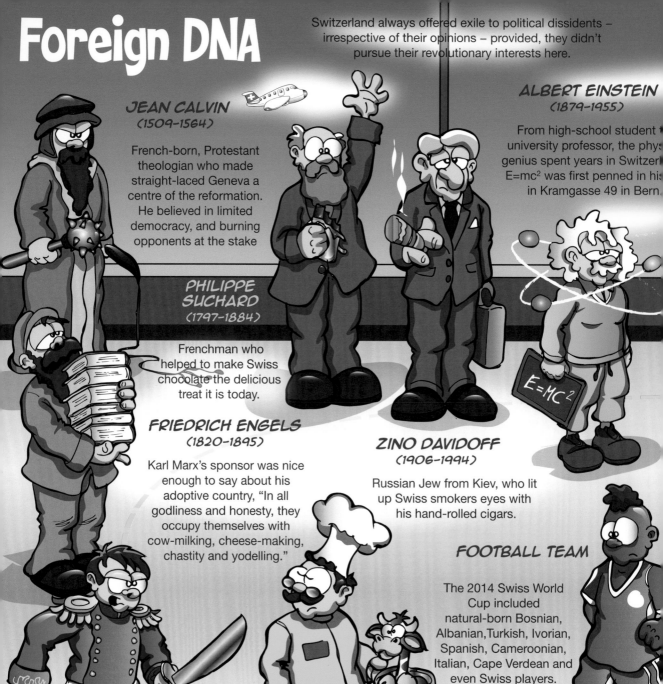

JEAN CALVIN
(1509-1564)

French-born, Protestant theologian who made straight-laced Geneva a centre of the reformation. He believed in limited democracy, and burning opponents at the stake

PHILIPPE SUCHARD
(1797-1884)

Frenchman who helped to make Swiss chocolate the delicious treat it is today.

ALBERT EINSTEIN
(1879-1955)

From high-school student university professor, the phys genius spent years in Switzer! $E=mc^2$ was first penned in his in Kramgasse 49 in Bern.

FRIEDRICH ENGELS
(1820-1895)

Karl Marx's sponsor was nice enough to say about his adoptive country, "In all godliness and honesty, they occupy themselves with cow-milking, cheese-making, chastity and yodelling."

ZINO DAVIDOFF
(1906-1994)

Russian Jew from Kiev, who lit up Swiss smokers eyes with his hand-rolled cigars.

FOOTBALL TEAM

The 2014 Swiss World Cup included natural-born Bosnian, Albanian, Turkish, Ivorian, Spanish, Cameroonian, Italian, Cape Verdean and even Swiss players.

GIUSEPPE MAZZINI
(1805-1872)

Italian freedom fighter who inspired Giuseppe Garibaldi. He orchestrated uprisings in Genoa and Savoy from his Geneva exile.

JULIUS MAGGI
(1846-1912)

The son of an Italian miller invented powdered soup and the stock cube.

NICOLAS HAYEK
(1928-2010)

The Lebanese Christian knew how his customers ticked he saved the Swiss watch industry with the Swatch.

NAPOLEON III. (1808–1873)

A citizen of Canton Thurgau, he hid near Lake Constance until the French republic demanded his extradition and threatened war with Switzerland. The emperor relocated to England.

ENNIS MIXED-TREBLE

er Federer (mother South African),
tina Hingis (mother Czech),
Wawrinka (father
man, granddad
sh).

VLADIMIR LENIN
(1870–1924)

Plotted both the Russian and the World Revolution from a two-room flat in Zurich's Spiegelgasse.

HEINRICH NESTLE
(1814–1890)

Chemist and political activist from Frankfurt, who found freedom and good fortune in Vevey with a frenchified name and his revolutionary milk powder.

CHARLES BROWN
(1863–1924)

WALTER BOVERI
(1865–1924)

The German engineers founded Switzerland's fifth largest company, the robotics and power conglomerate ABB.

JEAN-JACQUES ROUSSEAU
(1712–1778)

POLICE

The Frenchman sought freedom of thought and expression in Geneva. In Swiss peasants, he saw an example of the **noble savage**.

RELIGION

Neutral Switzerland has not been immune to Europe's history of religious strife. Protestant and Catholic cantons were at each other's throats for centuries . In 1597, matters of faith sundered Appenzell into Catholic Innerrhoden and Protestant Ausserrhoden.

Why all that zealotry? Maybe the country's location at the crossroads of Europe's religious divide. Or perhaps the fact that two influential reformers preached in Switzerland: Huldrych Zwingli (1484-1531) dominated Zurich, Jean Calvin (1509-1564) turned Geneva into the "Protestant Rome".

Today, Catholics make up 38% of Swiss believers, Protestants 26.1%. The third-largest group are non-believers with 22.2%, followed by Muslims (5.1%).

Islam is the most controversial religion. The Swiss have their share of radical Salafist preachers in various mosques, too. Mostly, these buildings lack minarets, since voters banned them in a referendum in 2009.

VERY SORRY, BUT IT SEEMS YOU FORGOT
TO PAY LAST YEAR'S CHURCH TAX!

SWISS HUMOUR

Sex

If you google "Swiss" and "sexy", two things happen: First, there's no prompt. Google just seems baffled by the suggestion. Second, among the top answers are adverts for a dieting pill ("Colon-fit") and "sexy and sustainable underwear".

If this confirms what you thought about Switzerland and sex, you're mistaken. There's more to it than meets the eye, both in theory and practice. When it comes to sex, the Swiss are like their lakes: still waters running deep.

Switzerland has traditionally been a leader in sexology, with medical institutes offering women courses in how to reach an orgasm. Not that many of them seem to need it: in the Durex Sexual Wellbeing Global Survey, the Swiss reliably come at the top in terms of frequency and satisfaction.

A ROOM FOR TWO

Extra-marital affairs are facilitated by a website ren out **Seitensprungzimme** literally: rooms for enjoyin bit on the side. More discr than a hotel and safer than conjugal bed.

BROTHELS

The vast majority are run by madames, not men. According to a study, they are overrun with job applications by ladies eager to work there: up to ten per week.

DRIVE-IN SEX

An innovative Zurich solution to combat prostitution by street-walkers: a garage-like shed hides a quick encounter in the client's car.

VENEREAL DISEASE

On the rise again after a short-lived slump. More than 350 new syphilis infections every year. For gonorrhea, twice as many.

31% of Swiss report using toys – lower than the Austr next door (43%).

HOMOSEXUALITY

Legal since 1942. Same-sex unions
were legalized in 2007

UNDERVALUED

In a survey, only 4% of people
around the world named
the Swiss as the best lovers.

CUCKOO CHILDREN

An estimated five
percent of all Swiss
kids are raised by a
man who's not their
biological father –
and has no idea.

HAPPY SWISS

70% of Swiss report being
sexually satisfied.

PROSTITUTION

Legal since 1942 and quite popular: an estimated 125 000 men regularly
visit one of the around 5000 hookers who work in more than 900
establishments. A high-end prostitute makes 1000 francs a day or more.

LITERATURE

She may only be a little girl, but just like her equally fictitious sisters Alice, Matilda, and Pippi Longstocking, Heidi has always been one of literature's most beloved and popular creations.

When Johanna Spyri published her novel about the orphan from the mountains, it was an instant hit – and has remained a bestseller ever since. With more than 50 million copies sold worldwide plus innumerable movies, cartoons and animes, Heidi is among the top ten best-selling books of all times.

Her success overshadows Switzerland's other contributions to world literature: Max Frisch, Friedrich Dürrenmatt, Charles Ramuz and Blaise Cendrars have significantly influenced German and French writing. London-based Alain de Botton might be Swiss, but the world regards him as essentially an English author.

Sadly, Swiss authors are little known in the English-speaking world. Germany, on the other hand, has fully embraced writers from their smaller neighbour as part of its own literary canon – from 19th century giants Wilhelm Raabe and Gottfried Keller through Frisch and Dürrenmatt to contemporaries Peter Stamm and wildly popular Martin Suter. So tight is this German inclusiveness, that occasionally those authors' Swiss origin is simply forgotten. Purely by accident, of course.

Art & Architecture

NIKI DE SAINT PHALLE
(1930-2002)

Big, fat, colourful women: Nana sculpture hovers under the roof of Zurich's main railway station.

MARIO BOTTA
(1943-)

San Francisco's landmark MoMA was conceived by the Ticino architect.

ARNOLD BÖCKLIN
(1827-1901)

Strange as it sounds, this master of symbolism inspired Dali.

JACQUES HERZOG (1950)
AND
PIERRE DE MEURON (1950)

Beijing's Bird's Nest Stadium is but one contemporary architectural icon created by the Basel duo.

This is a Church

ANGELIKA KAUFFMANN
(1741-1807)

She wasn't the only female painter, but until german Paula Modersohn-Becker, there was no one as famous as her.

HR GIGER
(1940-2014)

He's one of the scariest characters in Hollywood: the alien in the eponymous films. He was dreamed up by the mild-mannered surrealist painter HR Giger who got an Oscar for his creature.

OTHER ARCHITECTS

He built czar Peter the Great's new capital St. Petersburg: Domenico Trezzini (1670-1734)

Napoleon burnt Moscow down, Domenico Gilardi (1785-1845) helped rebuild it.

The only architect mentioned in Don Quixote: Giacomo Palearo (1520-1586) built fortresses in Pamplona, Mallorca and Lisbon.

FERDINAND HODLER
(1853–1918)

His **Woodcutter** still caused political controversy a century after it was painted when it was used in a political campaign.

PETER ZUMTHOR
(1943–)

Austere and strangely moving: acclaimed Therme Vals spa.

ALBERTO GIACOMETTI
(1901–1966)

Long, thin men, striding ahead with a purpose:

This is a church too

100 HELVETIA

AN TINGUELY
(1925–1991)

Crazy machines that make you smile and think.

HANS ERNI
(1909–2013)

Banknotes, posters and stamps carry his thumbprint.

LE CORBUSIER
(1887–1965)

He revolutionized architecture and still divides opinions with his stark, square buildings.

Customs and traditions

There is a school of thought which claims that a nation's emotional health is measured by how alive its customs and traditions are. If true, Switzerland needn't worry. According to the Federal Office for Culture, 167 ancient folk rites and practices are celebrated up and down the country. Even more remarkable: most of them have resisted attempts at commercialisation.

BASEL TATTOO

An example of Swiss successfully copying an original: now in its tenth year, the show is the world's second largest military tattoo after the famed Edinburgh event.

CHILBI

Raclette and rollercoasters, sausages and shooting galleries – autumn wouldn't be complete without the local fun fairs.

OLMA

Puts sleepy St. Gallen in the spotlight once a year. Conceived as an agricultural show in 1943, it has morphed into a big consumer fair. A highlight is the degustation hall, where you can sample treats, including the famous Olma bratwurst.

GENEVA ESCALADE

The Genevois celebrate their martyred heroes on 11-12 December, when they commemorate the citizens' defence against the Duke of Savoy's army in 1602. Festivities start with the ritual smashing of a pot made from chocolate to remember Mother Royaume. She slew an enemy soldier with a cast-iron kettle.

GANSABHAU

Central Swiss version piñata, played on Martin's day (11 Novemb Blindfolded contesta have to cut off the head strung up goo Fortunately, no real ge are used, but rather, v goose-shaped piña

CHALANDAMARZ

Cowbells and whips figure prominently at the beginning of March in canton Graubünden. School kids in traditional peasant's attire rampage through the villages. Their aim: to banish winter.

Fifes and drums, primeval masks, out of tune brass music, and even pole dancing – **Fasnacht** (carnival) means different things to different people in the country. Common to all is a seeming contradiction: having fun is taken seriously.

In April, uniformed members of Zurich's guilds parade through the city. The pageant ends at Sechseläuten Square, where a huge, explosives-filled wooden snowman is burnt. The sooner the **Böögg's** head explodes, so goes the legend, the hotter summer will be.

CHLAUS-CHLÖPFE

Between October and early December, it gets noisy in Lenzburg in canton Aarau, when whips up to five metres long are cracked day and night. This is supposed to wake up Santa who's sleeping in a nearby cave.

STREET-PARADE

A summer weekend of techno, dancing, and dehydration in Zurich city centre.

UNSPUNNENFEST

Swiss Olympics, featuring traditional Alpine games like stone toss and wrestling accompanied by yodels, alphorn and folk music. Comparable to the Scottish Highland Games.

CALIENTE !

Samba, tango, rumba: a new, hot and rather exotic tradition. Zurich hosts one of Europe's biggest festivals of Latin American music and culture.

BOY-SHOOTING (KNABENSCHIESSEN)

No children are hurt at this event, rather it's boys (and since 1991 girls) aged 13 to 17 who do the shooting. A serious contest with real weapons which gets increasingly (and worryingly for the boys) won by girls.

TRANSPORT

BISTRO

f God was a model rail enthusiast, he would play with Switzerland. Not just for the wonderful scenery, but for the network of trains, cable cars, buses, boats and Autobahns that crisscross the table – sorry, the country – with the beauty and precision of a well choreographed ballet.

A remarkable feat, considering that in transportational terms, Switzerland is a bit of a contradiction. On the one hand largely inaccessible due to its mountainous topography, on the other hand a major European thoroughfare due to its geographical centrality.

The Swiss quickly realized that there was money to be made out of this situation: they provided guides who safely led pilgrims, traders and soldiers over passes and through valleys. Over time, they improved travel arrangements – both for foreigners and themselves – by adding roads and railways, tunnels and bridges.

By now, there's hardly an inhabited place that cannot be reached by public transport, as every village with more than 100 citizens has a right to be connected to the network. And the train trip between Geneva and St. Gallen – the longest in the country – takes less than three hours.

Transportation

RAILWAYS

Switzerland's great love affair: Swiss railways SBB carry 1.2 million passengers per day in trains pulled by 700 engines over 5251 kilometres of track – through more than 80 major tunnels and over 8200 viaducts.

CARS

Less enjoyable, but still much enjoyed. Four million vehicles share 71 345 kilometres of road – albeit quite often standing still. There's an annual 40 franc toll for motorways.

PUBLIC TRANSPORT

Only Lausanne has a metro, all other cities mainly rely on their trusted and beloved tramways.

SHIPPING

The ships of 16 corporations ply the shores of Switzerland's bigger lakes – some are ferries, but most are pleasure craft. The US consul launched the first steamboat on Lake Geneva in 1823.

CABLE CARS, FUNICULARS AND COG RAILWAYS

A total of 588 aerial cableways, 12 cog railways and 53 funiculars open up the mountains. Bern's Marzili Funicular is the shortest (105 meters). The ten kilometre Jungfraujoch-Bahn cog railway takes you to 3454 meters above sea level, the highest in Europe.

R TRAVEL

National carrier Swiss and other airlines fly from three major hubs in Zurich, Geneva and Basel.

POSTBUS

Those magnificent men in their yellow machines, bus drivers are successors of intrepid coachmen. They ferry 140 million passengers yearly in 2193 buses over 869 routes – some of which scale vertiginous heights.

Railways

STEEPEST COG RAILWAY

Pilatusbahn
48% incline

ONCE UPON A TIME

The Swiss took late to railways, but once they started, they embraced them with a vengeance. The first trains came 1844 from Strasbourg and ended just outside Basel's city walls. Three years later, the first Swiss railroad spanned the 16 kilometres between Zurich and Baden. The 1860s saw a surge in construction as well as bankruptcies, as many private railway companies folded.

PUBLIC TRANSPORT STATIONS AND STOPS

2124

Tickets 1

Billette Billets Biglietti Tickets

DERAILMENTS (2015)

5

TICKETS

The Swiss relationship with trains has an erotic element, the GA amounts to tying the knot for life: a **Generalabonnement** (annual season-ticket) permits unlimited travel on almost all modes of public transport – trams, cable cars and boats included. Like a marriage, it comes at a price: CHF 3655 for second class, CHF 5970 for first. All the same, 460 000 people own one. Additionally, more than 2.3 million opt for the cheaper half-fare ticket at CHF 185.

GOTTHARD BASE TUNNEL

In 2016, the Swiss wrote railw. history when the **57 km** lon Gotthard Base Tunnel opened. the longest, deepest and flatte railway tunnel in the world ar promises to cut down travel tir between Zurich and Milan substantially.

NETWORK

The mountainous terrain proved difficult and only after Austria, France and Italy had traversed the Alps with tunnels, did Switzerland tackle the Gotthard crossing in 1882. After that, there was no looking back. Today, the **5252 km** long rail network includes some of the most spectacularly scenic routes in the world, such as the iconic Glacier Express between St. Moritz and Zermatt.

RAIL KM PER CAPITA PER YEAR

2307
(world's highest)

PUBLIC TRANSPORT EMPLOYEES

58 181

ALFRED ESCHER (1819-1882)

He was the rarest of beasts – a Swiss titan formed in the mould of the greatest 19th century American entrepreneurs. Politician, businessman and visionary, he single-handedly crafted the modern nation. He built the Gotthard tunnel, founded the country's best university (Zurich Polytechnic ETH), its second largest bank (today's Credit Suisse), and largest insurer (Swiss Life). He is one of the very few Swiss to be honoured with a monument – fittingly outside Zurich railway station.

PUNCTUALITY

Some Swiss get mad when their train is just two minutes late. However, it's not necessarily a sign of a disturbing fixation with punctuality. For if their connecting train or bus leaves on time, two minutes can turn into a much longer delay. Swiss rail SBB claims to be on time 97 per cent of the time – meaning, not more than three minutes late.

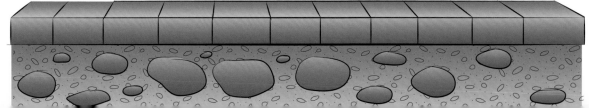

CARS

If Swiss are so good at making things, why don't they produce cars? Unfortunately, after some promising attempts in automobiles' infant years, Swiss producers concentrated on pimping, sorry: improving, other makes.

Enter Peter Monteverdi, who in 1954 inherited his father's garage outside Basel. Ten years later he built luxury sports cars, which he named after himself. The company stopped production in 1990.

Wim Oubouter, however, follows the road of improving other makers' designs. With the Microlino he introduced a modern, electric version of the legendary 1950s "bubble car".

But who needs a car industry, if one of America's most iconic automobiles has a Swiss pedigree: the Chevy. Swiss racing driver Louis Chevrolet co-founded the company in 1911. Even the bowtie logo is said to be a modified Swiss cross.

EDUCATION

There's probably no company where a Swiss feels less at ease than among Americans. Their ingrained habit of blowing their own trumpet runs against all his instincts, his upbringing and his identity, which all scream understatement.

To sell themselves short is second nature to the Swiss, which has – unfairly – given rise to the suspicion that they must be a bit dumb. Among Germans, this false impression is further strengthened by their idiosyncratic Swiss German dialect.

Nothing could be further from the truth. The Swiss are among the world's best educated people: one third of the population gains a university degree at one of the country's 12 universities. An impressive 86 percent finish high school or complete vocational training. Even more astonishing: 3.2 percent earn a PhD.

Switzerland's educational system is solidly built from the bottom up: pre-school, primary, secondary, tertiary, university. There are many diverging paths, where one can choose a different route best suited to one's own interests and capabilities. Switzerland's apprenticeship system is the envy of most of the developed world.

Schooling has been compulsory since 1874, based on the radical notion that "people's education is people's liberation". Geneva introduced mandatory education as early as 1536, followed by Bern (1615) and Zurich (1637).

One of the most influential educational reformers was Johann Heinrich Pestalozzi (1746-1827) who revolutionized the way children were taught. He ruled that head, heart and hands should be equally stimulated – intellect, morals and dexterity.

Education

Kindergarten

Primary

Lower Secondary

COMPULSORY EDUCATION

Primary school starts at age 6 and it is only here when pupils learn to read and write – late by Anglo-Saxon standards, but Swiss educators insist no evidence has been found that Swiss kids have been hurt by all that playing.

Lower secondary school generally lasts 3 years and in most cantons students are streamed into performance-based groups. This is the end of compulsory education.

23 year old

15 year old

12 year old

KINDERGARTEN

Kindergarten lasts two years, is compulsory in most cantons, and generally begins at age 4.

8 year old

3 year old

PRIVATE SCHOOLS

Only 5% of students go to private schools

Ticino offers a pre-kindergarten for 3-year-olds, the only canton to do so.

VOCATIONAL TRAINING

During the 3 to 5 year apprenticeship, pupils have the possibility to complete the vocational baccalaureate, allowing entry to the universities of applied science.

Upper Secondary

There is a dizzying array of upper secondary school options in Switzerland, from baccalaureate schools (Gymnasia), to business and specialised schools, as well as dance, music and, of course, hospitality.

HIGH SCHOOL EXIT EXAM

MATURA

Tertiary

45% of adults obtain a tertiary education degree or diploma, 30% from a university, 15% from an institution of professional education and training.

Ongoing

Switzerland is a top choice for professionals and students from around the world for ongoing academic, business, and professional development.

DIPLOMA

Berufsmatura

THE VERY BEST

Switzerland's vocational apprenticeship system is the envy of the world, with roughly two-thirds of Swiss students combining classroom instruction at a vocational school with an apprenticeship in a training company (dual-track system).

VETERINARY FACULTY

ADMISSIONS

ANIMALS PREFER SWISS DOCTORS

Generally, Swiss universities are open to foreign students, assuming that their high school qualifications are recognized by Switzerland. One exception is veterinary medicine. Applicants from EU countries may only apply after they've completed five semesters at home. Non-Europeans must have lived at least five years in Switzerland. Surely, it can't be the concern about language problems between patients and doctors?

VOCATIONAL TRAINING

If you're a butcher, a banker, or maybe even a candlestick maker – learning a trade is a serious business in Switzerland and all trades enjoy high social standing. Experts from the US have been beating a path to Switzerland's door to study its vocational training concept – called the **dual system**. *Apprentices learn at a workshop and attend classes at a vocational college at the same time. This gives them a well-rounded education and a high level of confidence in their job. They can also prepare for the* **Matura** *university entrance exams.*

SCIENCE

MRS. KAUF? IT SEEMS THAT WE'VE LOST YOUR HUSBAND
IN A BLACK HOLE WE ACCIDENTALLY CREATED...

...NO, WE DON'T KNOW IF HE'LL BE BACK ANYTIME SOON.

What do Velcro, Schweppes, the garlic press and Ritalin have in common? They are all Swiss inventions, along with countless others, including DDT, LED and LSD – for insects, lights and psychedelic trips respectively. Whether mundane (sugar cubes), musical (Rickenbacher`s e-guitars) or momentous (Theory of Relativity) – Swiss scientists have changed our lives considerably.

Much of it was developed in some Swiss precursor to Bill Gates's famous garage: a hut with a work bench. But science and research is heavily promoted by the government, too – to the tune of 2.1 billion francs per year.

This explains why this small nation boasts 21 Nobel laureates in medicine, chemistry and physics. Not included are foreigners who studied at a Swiss university: Wilhelm Röntgen, Albert Einstein and Wolfgang Pauli to name but a few.

In the Global Innovation Index, which measures a nation's ability to forge ahead intellectually, Switzerland reliably finishes in first place – well ahead of R&D power houses such as Japan, the US or Germany. China doesn't even make it to the first two dozen countries.

Two of the world's current most ambitious scientific projects are also based in Switzerland. CERN's Large Hadron Collider tries to figure out the trifling matter of the universe's basic make-up. The Human Brain Project at Lausanne's university attempts a complete computer simulation of the human brain.

Both projects smack of human hubris, of a desire to play at being God. How sensible then, to entrust them to the pragmatic Swiss.

Inventions

ELECTRIC GUITAR

The first ones, in the 1930s, were called **Frying Pans** – because that was what they looked like. Still, Adolph Rickenbacher's invention was an instant success – and changed the way we listen to music forever.

PRE-FAB CONCRETE

Once derided as the ugly face of Socialist architecture, pre-fab concrete housing estates were actually a Swiss invention. Ernst Göhner built thousands of affordable apartments in the 1960s all around Zurich.

VELCRO

Avid hiker Georges de Mestral was annoyed by pesky burrs that got stuck to his walking socks and his dog's fur. But when he looked closer he saw a modern alternative to the zip. Velcro was born in 1948.

LSD

Pharmacist Albert Hofmann stumbled onto a strange new compound in 1948. Undaunted, he tried it on himself – and liked it. So did a generation of psychedelic hippies years later.

NESCAFÉ

When Brazil was suffering from a glut of coffee beans in the 1920s, they turned for help to Nestlé company in Vevey. Their chemist Max Morgenthaler found a way to store coffee almost indefinitely without losing its taste.

MATHEMATICS

Differential equations, probability, calculus, fluid dynamics and important symbols like Σ, π or $f(x)$ – the world of mathematics is unthinkable without Swiss contribution, especially by the redoubtable Bernoulli family and their 18th century contemporary Leonhard Euler.

RORSCHACH TEST

A plain inkblot can open the doors to a person's psyche: the Freudian psychoanalyst Hermann Rorschach developed the simple but effective test that was named after him.

COMPUTER MOUSE

Navigating a computer screen was quite a challenge for a long time. René Sommer changed all that in the 1980s with the first computer mouse.

MICROSCOOTER

didn't like to walk to the station
d didn't fancy riding a bike all the
y to work. So Wim Oubouter
ne up with the microscooter – fast
d foldable.

STOCK CUBE

A simple and nourishing food for factory workers – this was Julius Maggi's starting point in the 1870s. He developed packet soup, the famous Maggi sauce, and eventually the trusted stock cube.

ZIPPER

Generations of inventors had tried and failed to come up with a fail-safe way to fasten clothes. But only Martin Winterhalter succeeded in the 1930s. His zip is basically the same we use today.

CELLOPHANE

A spilled glass of wine not only angered Jacques Edwin Baumgartner but also set him thinking: he wanted some water-repellent material to protect his favourite tablecloth. In 1908 he patented cellophane.

ROBIDOG

A very Swiss invention: special receptacles for dumping dog poo.
Unmistakable in their bright green livery, they're virtually everywhere.
Except, when you need one. They're being phased out gradually.
Henceforth, excreta will go into regular bins.

INNOVATION

There are countries so fertile – you drop a cherry stone and end up with an orchard. Others float on oceans of crude or natural gas.

The Swiss are not so blessed: they have mostly a thin layer of hardscrabble pastures, covering plain rock. However, they often left inventing things from scratch to others. They concentrated on substantially improving products – from cheese to smashing atoms.

Sitting pretty: in 1905, Albert Emil Gebert invented the toilet cistern. Today, his company is a global market leader, making the competition flush.

Science

AUGUSTE PICCARD (1884-1962)
Scaled heights as well as depths. With a balloon he rose to 23 000 meters, his bathyscape dived 4176 meters into the sea. His real fame was elsewhere: he was the inspiration for Tintin's Professor Calculus.

CERN

Where sub-atomic particles are taken for a spin – 100 meters underground inside a 27– kilometer long circular tunnel. Established 1954, more than 12 000 scientists, fellows and associates work for the European Organisation for Nuclear Research.

PARACELSUS (1493-1541)
Groundbreaking medieval doctor, founder of toxicology, inventor of laudanum.

DNA

He found the first clue to decode the human genome: Friedrich Miescher (1844-1895) isolated nucleic acids, the basis for DNA.

PSYCHO-ANALYSIS

If Sigmund Freud is the master, Carl Jung (1875-1961) is his most influential student. The younger man continued Freud's work and founded analytical psychology.

WORLD WIDE WEB

Granted, Tim Berners-Lee was British. But he invented it while working at CERN in Geneva. His first web server, the NeXT machine, is still there.

HUMAN BRAIN PROJECT

How does the grey matter inside our skulls work? The EU's ambitious project is coordinated by Lausanne's technical university.

JACQUES PICCARD (1922-2008)
The son went even deeper than the father – 10 911 meters to the bottom of the Mariana trench in the Pacific Ocean.

ALBERT EINSTEIN (1879-1955) First jotted down the world's most famous equation in his flat in Bern. Following his studies in Zurich, he became a Swiss citizen.

BERTRAND PICCARD (1958-)
His son, took to the air again: he twice went around the globe – first in a balloon, then in a solar-powered aircraft.

NOBEL PRIZES

All in all 26 have been awarded to Swiss, most of them – 20 – in natural sciences and medicine. Remarkable for such a small country: Spain, Japan, Italy and even China have fewer.

NIKLAUS WIRTH
(1968) inventor of computer language Pascal.

$E = MC^2$

PASCAL

KARL ALEXANDER MÜLLER
Nobel prize in physics for high-temperature superconductivity

ROLF MARTIN ZINKERNAGEL
Nobel prize in medicine for a breakthrough in immunology

KURT WÜTHRICH
Nobel prize in chemistry for biological macromolecules.

HEINRICH ROHRER
Nobel prize in physics for microscope that can see at atomic level.

PAUL KARRER
Nobel prize in chemistry for work in vitamins.

LAST
(BUT NOT LEAST)

THANK YOU NOTE...

The authors of this book will like to acknowledge the help of the following kind people who in many different ways helped us in the making of this book:

Richard Harvell - Anja Kauf - Miguel Lievano - Andrea Larry - Oberst René Meier - Oberstlt Yves Reber - Wim Ouboter - Anita Oswald - Stephan Kauf - Marianne Oswald

Also, thank you to everyone on the Bergli Books team, including Markus Moser, Laurent Gachnang, Satu Binggeli, Nora Schmid, Tharsana Selvaratnam, Frank Deppeler, Kimberly Smith, Ruedi Bienz, Thomas Gierl, Liv Etienne, Sarah Bislin, Annette Eichholz und Alexandra Mendez-Diez.

The Authors

SERGIO J. LIEVANO

If you grow up on a coffee farm in the Colombian Andes, Switzerland is probably not the first country on your radar – except, perhaps, as a far-away mythical place, where people are always on time, traffic lights are more than street decorations and politicians are not magicians who mastered the art of vanishing big chunks of the national GDP. So, for Sergio it took some time and detours before he found both his true calling and the country of his heart. He studied economics in Bogotá, then – rather listlessly – worked for a flavours and fragrance company, before sharpening his wits and pens to start drawing cartoons and publishing books.

When he met his Swiss wife Anja, everything fell into place, and Sergio fully embraced Switzerland, his spouse and his kids. Five books on Switzerland, including the bestselling Hoi saga, are the results of this labour of love, but nothing prepared him for the encounter with Wolfgang, the Teuton, with his Germanic zest for order and timeliness. Sergio's passion for Switzerland is strongly connected to his muse, Anja, and his three most ardent fans and toughest critics: his kids. Helping to set things right, in a thoroughly Swiss fashion.

WOLFGANG KOYDL

His little sister loved Heidi, he read Schiller's play Wilhelm Tell in German lit classes, and as a special treat there was the occasional piece of Swiss chocolate. Other than that, Switzerland could have been on a different planet when Wolfgang grew up in Bavaria. Road and rail connections were almost medievally slow and cumbersome (come to think of it, they still are). It also was a rather expensive planet, as Wolfgang's father always reminded his family when holiday destinations were discussed: "you want mountains, we got our own."

In subsequent decades, Wolfgang and Switzerland continued to move in different orbits: Wolfgang working as a foreign newspaper correspondent for the German wire service dpa and for Süddeutsche Zeitung in Egypt, Russia, Turkey, the US and the United Kingdom, while Switzerland remained more or less stationary. Until Süddeutsche decided to dispatch him to that enigmatic little nation in the mountains. Since then, he hasn't looked back, covering – and often personally experiencing – everything from Alpine wrestling to yodelling. After several books (Wer hats erfunden, Die Besserkönner, Die Bessermacher), in which he tried to plumb the depths of the Swiss soul and character, he decided to join forces with Sergio Lievano, probably the shrewdest illustrator of Swiss particularities and sensibilities. Perhaps together, they'll succeed into pulling this exciting planet closer to the rest of humanity.

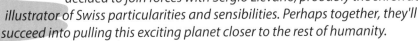

ABOUT BERGLI BOOKS

Since 1988, Bergli Books has been publishing books in Switzerland that bridge intercultural gaps. Its mostly-English list has included many Swiss-interest bestsellers of the past two decades, including the Ticking Along Series, Margaret Oertig's Beyond Chocolate, and Sergio Lievano and Nicole Egger's Hoi books—the bestselling Swiss German guides of all time. An imprint of the world's oldest publisher, Schwabe Publishing, Bergli is unique in Switzerland—connecting English readers to Swiss culture and tradition.

Swiss German Survival

Four editions of the singular,
best-selling Swiss German survival
guide

HOI –
YOUR NEW SWISS GERMAN SURVIVAL GUIDE

by **Sergio J. Lievano** and **Nicole Egger** (Swiss German / Zürich dialect – English edition).
ISBN 978-3-905252-67-5.

SALI ZÄMME –
YOUR BASELDÜTSCH SURVIVAL GUIDE

by **Sergio J. Lievano** and **Nicole Egger**.
Basel dialect ISBN 978-3-905252-26-2.

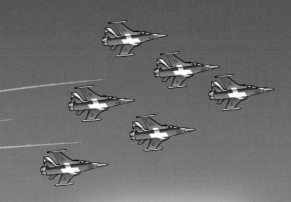

HOI ET APRÈS...
MANUEL DE SURVIE EN SUISSE ALLEMAND

by **Sergio J. Lievano** and **Nicole Egger.**
(Zürich dialect – French edition of Hoi)
ISBN 978-3-905252-16-3.

HOI ZÄME –
SCHWEIZERDEUTSCH LEICHT GEMACHT

von **Sergio J. Lievano** und **Nicole Egger**
Macht mit seinen über 200 witzigen und farbenfrohen Cartoons das Erlernen der Sprache zu einem vergnüglichen Erlebnis.
ISBN 978-3-905252-22-4.

The End

FOLLOW US !